# Annapolis

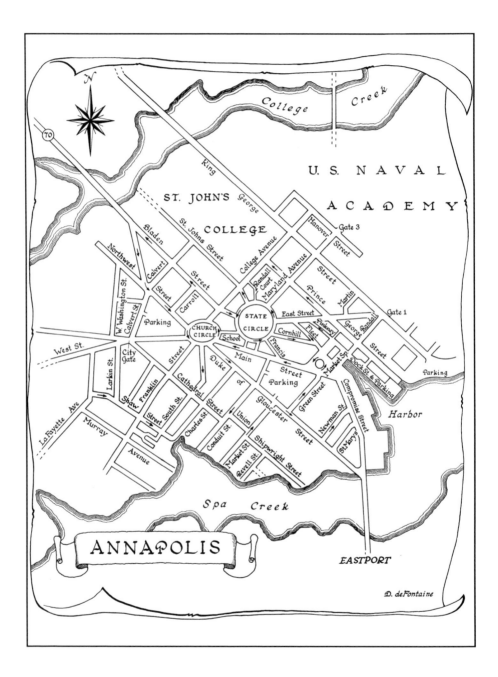

ANNAPOLIS

# *Annapolis*
## A Walk Through History

### Elizabeth B. Anderson
*With Michael P. Parker*

Photographs by
## M. E. Warren

TIDEWATER PUBLISHERS
A Division of Schiffer Publishing, Ltd.
Atglen, Pennsylvania

ISBN: 978-0-87033-546-4

Published by Schiffer Publishing, Ltd.
4880 Lower Valley Road
Atglen, PA 19310
Phone: (610) 593-1777; Fax: (610) 593-2002
E-mail: Info@schifferbooks.com

For our complete selection of fine books on this and related subjects, please visit our website at www.schifferbooks.com. You may also write for a free catalog.

The maps are adapted from those by D. de Fontaine in *Colonial Annapolis, 1694–1972*, copyright © 1971 by Robert Barton.

Library of Congress Cataloging-in-Publication Data

Anderson, Elizabeth B. (Elizabeth Blessing)
  Annapolis : a walk through history / Elizabeth B. Anderson, with Michael P.
  Parker ;  photographs by  M. E. Warren.— 2nd ed.
       p. cm.
Includes bibliographical references and index.
  ISBN 978-0-87033-546-4 (pbk.)
  1. Historic buildings—Maryland—Annapolis—Guidebooks. 2. Annapolis
(Md.)—Tours. 3. Walking—Maryland—Annapolis (Md.)—Guidebooks. 4.
Annapolis (Md.)—Buildings, structures, etc.—Guidebooks. 5.
Architecture—Maryland—Annapolis—Guidebooks. I. Parker, Michael P.
II. Title.
  F189.A68 A23 2003
  917.52'56—dc22
                                    2003015850

Printed in China
First edition, 1984. Second edition, 2003. Second printing 2015

# Contents

# List of Illustrations

# Foreword

As I walk through the streets of an old town, whether as a visitor or an inhabitant, I cannot help wondering about the buildings. I want to know when they were built, what purpose they served, and what styles of architecture they represent. Even more, I want to know about the people who built and occupied them, for as Shakespeare said (in *Coriolanus*), "What is the city but the people?"

Without inhabitants, a city is but an aggregation of bricks and mortar, a theater, a stage, waiting for the actors to make their entrance. I cannot help wondering who peopled it in times past, what their hopes and fears were, how they lived, and what they thought about God and man, and about life, liberty, and the pursuit of happiness.

The visitor to Annapolis who is not acquainted with the historical background is limited to what elementary conjecture affords about Annapolitans of yesteryear. There are, of course, books and excellent guided tours available. But how can a visitor on his or her own identify the material remains of the past and appreciate the folk who lived and moved and had their being here? The answer is to carry a good guidebook while threading one's way through the historic district that is beautiful downtown Annapolis.

I remember the excitement I derived, forty-odd years ago, from a small guidebook by the late Henry Sturdy, a knowledgeable local historian whom I later had the pleasure of knowing. As I walked the brick sidewalks of Annapolis, buckled here and there by overgrown roots of ancient trees, the past came alive in my imagination, and Carrolls, Dulanys, and Ridouts, as well as butchers, bakers, and candlestickmakers, seemed once more to be about their business— like the one day each century when Brigadoon resurfaces!

Annapolis has been without an up-to-date guidebook for a number of years. As one who loves the old town and wishes to share his affection for it with others, I have regretted this fact and longed to see someone fill the breach. Mrs. Anderson has done so. She has written what I regard as an excellent one, and I commend it to you.

Arthur Pierce Middleton

# Acknowledgments

I dedicate this effort most especially to my friend Audrey Ewald, who never doubted I would finish it. And to Dee Buinicki, who wasn't so sure, but supported me nonetheless. My family has seen me start many projects, only to be discouraged when they took too long. To Dick, who has the only business head among us and also types; to Liz, who despaired of my syntax; to Ned, who is always supportive of his mom; and to Jon, who only reads my books between the covers. And finally, to Mike Parker, without whom there would have been no book.

I should also like to acknowledge the help of many other people, but I can only name a few. I wish to thank Paula Fishback and Norma Grovermann, who allowed my imagination to flourish while I was learning about three centuries of Annapolis history, and Barbara Brand, who helped me refine that knowledge at the Hammond-Harwood House. My friends on the staff at the Hammond-Harwood House, especially Sam and Helen Nichols and Emmy Lou Dicken, must be thanked. Barry Burrows sent me to my publisher. And Dr. Arthur Middleton was so encouraging in his comments and editorial work. I also want to thank my readers, Barbara Brand and Harry Ewald, who caught small errors. I must also acknowledge the resources of the Maryland Historical Trust and its staff, which allowed me free rein in the Historic American Buildings Survey. To all, my heartfelt appreciation.

As I began my work on the second edition of this book I called on my Annapolis friend Penny Evans to give me some current information which I could not glean from research. She was always helpful and gave me great encouragement for this long-distance project. Many thanks.

*The publisher wishes to acknowledge the assistance of Donna C. Hole, Chief of Historic Preservation, and Mariah McGunigle of the City of Annapolis Department of Planning and Zoning, who reviewed the new edition of* Annapolis *using recent architectural research.*

# Annapolis

# A City Steeped in History

The early history of Annapolis is intimately bound to that of Maryland, and it is with the planting of the first colony at St. Mary's City in 1634 that the story of Annapolis begins. Prior to that time, George Calvert, the founder of Maryland, served as secretary of state and member of the privy council in England during the reign of James I. Although born an Anglican, Calvert had converted to Catholicism; since Catholics were legally prohibited from holding public office, Calvert kept his religious beliefs private until 1625 when he disclosed his conversion to the king. He resigned as secretary of state soon after, but James I, in compensation for Calvert's services and as a measure of his continued esteem, named him Baron Baltimore in the Irish peerage. With the death of James I in 1625, Calvert retired from public life.

In 1623 Calvert had received a patent to found a colony at Avalon in Newfoundland. He visited the plantation in 1627 but found the climate so severe that he applied to the new sovereign, Charles I, for a grant of land in the warmer territories of Virginia. The new patent was issued in June 1632, but since Lord Baltimore died in April of that year, the colony was granted instead to his eldest son and heir, Cecil, the second Lord Baltimore.

Under the leadership of Cecil's brother Leonard Calvert, 150 settlers were dispatched to Maryland in November 1633 in two ships, *Ark* and *Dove*. The party landed at St. Clement's Island on the Potomac on March 25, 1634, and established the settlement of St. Mary's. Although the Calverts had envisioned Maryland as a sanctuary for persecuted Catholics, more than half of the original settlers were communicants of the Anglican Church.

Despite the enactment of a statute in 1649 guaranteeing religious toleration, the animosities between Anglicans, Puritans, and Catholics that had afflicted England throughout the seventeenth century soon were evident in the New World as well.

The new colony and its capital at St. Mary's prospered. In 1649 the provincial legislature welcomed a group of Puritan refugees from Virginia. Governor William Stone granted them land on the Severn River in the newly organized Anne Arundel County. Under their leader Richard Bennett, the Puritans founded a settlement named Providence located on Greenbury Point, now the site of Annapolis Naval Station. What is today downtown Annapolis was granted to Thomas Todd, who christened the tract Todd's Landing. The English Civil War and the execution of King Charles I fomented disputes between the Calverts' Catholic proprietary government and the Protestant Puritans of Providence. When Oliver Cromwell became Lord Protector in England, the Puritans challenged the authority of Maryland's Catholic government by refusing the oath of loyalty to the proprietor, prompting Governor Stone to lead an expedition to subdue the hostile settlement. On March 25, 1655, his troops met the citizens of Providence in battle at Horn Point, in present-day Eastport. Stone was captured and twenty of his men slain; this victory ensured Puritan ascendancy in the colony for the next two years.

In 1657, Lord Baltimore reached an accord with Cromwell and reasserted his control over Maryland. Religious disputes took a back seat to economic issues for thirty years and Providence—then called "the town at Proctor's" after Robert Proctor, who purchased Todd's Landing—slowly grew into a tobacco-shipping port. With the accession of the Catholic King James II to the throne in 1685, however, political anarchy once again threatened Maryland. James was overthrown by his Anglican daughter Mary and her Dutch husband William of Orange in the Glorious Revolution in 1688. Protestant Marylanders led by a St. Mary's planter, John Coode, took their cue from English events and overthrew the government of the Catholic Calverts in 1689. "The Association in arms, for the defence of the Protestant religion," as the rebels called themselves, appealed to England for support, and King William responded in 1691 by annulling the Calvert charter and declaring Maryland a royal colony. He dispatched Sir Lionel Copley as governor. Copley died in 1693 and was succeeded by Francis Nicholson, who had been serving as lieutenant governor of Virginia.

At the urging of Nicholson, the Maryland Assembly voted in 1694 to remove the capital of Maryland from St. Mary's to Anne-Arundel Towne, which in the following year was renamed Annapolis after Princess Anne, the sister of Queen Mary. Nicholson's rationale for moving the capital was that Annapolis provided a more central location; another motivation, however, was religious, for the largely Catholic population of St. Mary's harbored sympathy for the ousted Calverts. Nicholson awarded contracts for the building of a church, a state house, and a school, and he laid out the baroque street plan that still distinguishes Annapolis today. In 1697 a visitor reported that Annapolis could boast "40 Dwelling Houses . . . 7 or 8 [of] which can afford a good Lodging and accommodations for strangers." Nicholson left Annapolis in 1698 on his appointment as governor of Virginia, where he founded Williamsburg. It was lamented that "had governour Nicholson continu'd there [in Annapolis] a few Years longer, he had brought it to Perfection."

Despite this auspicious beginning, it was nearly a half-century before Annapolis began to assume the character for which it is known. The streets were unpaved and unlighted; pigs and cows roamed at will; tanneries rendered the air somewhat less than salubrious. When the state house burned in 1704, the resulting loss of all land records touched off a legal crisis that brought building to a stop. Ebenezer Cooke, the unofficial poet laureate of Maryland, described Annapolis in *The Sot-Weed Factor* (1708) as

> A city situate on a plain
> Where scarce a house will keep out rain;
> The buildings framed with cypress rare
> Resemble much our Southwick fair;
> But strangers there will scarcely meet
> With market place, exchange, or street;
> And if the truth I may report,
> It's not so large as Tottenham Court.

In all respects Annapolis seemed to have been a rough-and-ready outpost of the British Empire. Two factors, however, ensured its growth. First, its position as the colonial capital necessitated the presence of fledgling bureaucracy; the meetings of the Maryland Assembly spurred a proliferation of taverns, inns, and small service businesses. Second, the 1694 designation of Annapolis as the port of entry for the upper Chesapeake Bay made the city a thriving port. In the early years of the eighteenth century tobacco was the main export. Ships carrying manufactured articles and luxury goods from England and Scotland would unload their merchandise in Annapolis and return to Europe filled with tobacco. Between 1748 and 1775 an average of slightly over 7,300 hogsheads of tobacco cleared customs in Annapolis each year. As the eighteenth century progressed, wheat from the valleys of central Maryland formed a larger percentage of the colony's exports; pig iron smelted in Baltimore and Anne Arundel Counties also grew in importance. Annapolis simultaneously became the distribution center for European goods: 83,000 gallons of rum, for example, were landed in 1755 alone. The famed capacity of Annapolitans notwithstanding, much of this rum was presumably shipped to other parts of the colony.

Colonial commerce and the plantation system, however, had a dark side. The English ships that docked in Annapolis carried not only goods but also slaves and indentured servants. In January 1748, for example, Captain Willock Macky of the schooner *John and Mildred* advertised that he had landed in Annapolis with a cargo that included coffee, chocolate, sugar, shoes, and "one young Negro Man, and two Women, etc., very reasonable for ready Money." The ship *Randolph* out of Bristol in 1766 carried "EIGHTY CONVICT SERVANTS, Men and Women; amongst which there are several TRADESMEN, and to be Sold on Board the Ship, now lying in the Dock." Although many indentured servants eventually bought their freedom and often became citizens of substance, their period of servitude was rarely easy. The lot of the slave, no matter how kind his owner, was worse. The trade in indentured servants ended with the Revolution; the slavery upon which so much of the prosperity of Annapolis was built persisted for another ninety years.

The golden age of Annapolis occurred in the fifteen years preceding the Revolution. In 1754 Thomas Pownall wrote that

> the original plan of the town was laid in circular streets,
> with cross streets running from the centre like radii. The
> State House, Governor's House, Assembly, Courts, etc.,
> were to have formed the centre, at the top of the hill,
> with concentral streets going round the hill; but the town
> is far from being compleat, nor do the traces of such a
> plan appear in what is built; it makes a very irregular appearance, and is in size and form but a very poor town.

By 1769, however, William Eddis could report

> the buildings of Annapolis were formerly of small dimensions and of inelegant construction; but there are now
> several modern edifices which make a good appearance.
> There are few habitations without gardens, some of which

are planted in a decent style and are well stocked. At present, this city has more the appearance of an agreeable village than a metropolis of an opulent province, as it contains within its limits a number of small fields which are intended for future erections.

What had occurred in the interim between Pownall's visit and Eddis's arrival from England was a building boom of unanticipated proportions. In the 1760s families like the Brices, the Pacas, the Scotts, and the Ridouts erected their imposing town houses. The "future erections" predicted by Eddis would include the Dulany House on Duke of Gloucester Street and those most elegant of Annapolis residences, the Chase-Lloyd House and the Hammond-Harwood House, both on Maryland Avenue.

This architectural renaissance was just one of the manifestations of the new social spirit engendered by prosperity. Eddis, who came to Annapolis to serve as secretary to Governor Robert Eden, records a heady round of balls, card parties, and fetes during the winter season when planters flocked to Annapolis for sittings of the Assembly and the proprietary courts. Horse races were held at the track outside the City Gate and later in Parole. The theater erected on West Street in 1771 produced the staples of the London stage. Annapolis society danced at the Assembly Rooms on Duke of Gloucester Street. Clubs proliferated: the Jockey Club, the Tuesday Club, the Forensic Club, and the South River Club. Under the editorship of Jonas Green, the *Maryland Gazette* kept Annapolitans up-to-date on politics, literature, and London tobacco prices. Annapolis society grew refined without losing touch with the countryside that supplied its wealth; the ability to judge good horseflesh remained as much the mark of a gentleman as the inclination to "dispute upon the quality of Latin vowels." Eddis's commendation of the "polished society" of Annapolis is supported by the observations of the Reverend Jonathan Boucher, rector of St. Anne's, who remarked in April 1770 that Annapolis was "the genteelest town in North America."

Annapolitans took a prominent part in the political controversies that preceded the outbreak of the American Revolution. King George I had restored Maryland to the Calvert family in 1715. Annapolitans opposed the imposition of the Stamp Act of 1765 on unusual grounds: eschewing the philosophical arguments of their peers in Virginia and New England, Marylanders maintained that the colony's charter empowered the proprietor alone to impose new taxes. Formal Maryland opposition to the Crown took this legalistic tack until the actual overthrow of the proprietary government in 1775. Revolutionary fervor nevertheless began to flicker among the Annapolis citizenry throughout the early 1770s. The Sons of Liberty met by torchlight under the old tulip poplar on the St. John's College campus. In 1774 a mob burned the brig *Peggy Stewart* off Windmill Point in Spa Creek after its owner, Anthony Stewart of Hanover Street, paid the detested tax on the small amount of tea in its cargo. In June 1776 Governor Eden was permitted to leave the city on the British frigate *Fowey* after the revolutionary authorities rejected the demands of Virginia that he be imprisoned. Eden, who was extremely popular among Annapolitans, returned to Maryland after the war; he died in 1783 at the Upton Scott House on Shipwright Street.

The four Marylanders who signed the Declaration of Independence—William Paca, Thomas Stone, Samuel Chase, and Charles Carroll of Carrollton—all had ties with Annapolis. Sometime during their varied careers, all four owned homes in Annapolis, and the buildings are still standing. Despite periodic panics touched off by British warships patrolling the Bay, Annapolis saw no combat during the Revolution; from the earthworks of Fort Severn, constructed on Windmill Point, a shot was never fired. Only with the final campaign of the Revolution did the war come close to home: General Rochambeau and his troops arrived in Annapolis in October 1781 en route to Yorktown. The force encamped on the shores of College Creek before it embarked on ships for the final battle of the Revolution.

In 1783 the Continental Congress, which had recently adjourned in Princeton, accepted the invitation to reconvene in Annapolis in November of that year. Two events of moment occurred during the nine-month session: George Washington resigned his commission as commander in chief of the Continental Army at the State House on December 23, 1783; and the Treaty of Paris, which brought the Revolutionary War to an end, was ratified in early 1784. Therefore, Annapolis served as the capital of the United States between November 26, 1783, and August 13, 1784.

Annapolis would see yet one more meeting of the representatives from the other colonies when a constitutional convention convened in September 1786. Several of the colonies, including Maryland itself, were unrepresented due to political disputes, and the delegates voted to reassemble in Philadelphia the following May. It was this convention in 1787 that drafted the Constitution of the United States and the Bill of Rights.

The political importance of Annapolis during the 1780s could not obscure the fact that its economic preeminence in Maryland had slowly slipped away. Baltimore, with its deepwater harbor and easy access to western markets, had already overtaken Annapolis as a center of commerce. Although Annapolis continued to grow after the Revolution, by 1793 it had ceased all aspirations regarding major international trade and had gradually faded into a sleepy market town, mainly tied to the surrounding agricultural districts. A number of Annapolis families relocated to Baltimore, which soon became the social center of the state. By 1804 an English visitor, Sir Augustus Foster, could remark sorrowfully that "the best society used to be found here a few years back." Only the presence of the state government continued to testify to the city's former importance—it remained in Annapolis to placate rural interests despite repeated efforts to move the capital to Baltimore.

The early years of the nineteenth century were a quiet period for Annapolis. Although the outbreak of the War of 1812 sent citizens scurrying to refortify Fort Severn and to construct the new Fort Madison on the north shore of the river, the British fleet that harried the Chesapeake under Admiral Cockburn in 1813 and 1814 never even attempted a landing at Annapolis, perhaps an indication of the city's relative unimportance at this time. During the bombardment of Fort McHenry in September 1814, Francis Scott Key, a graduate of St. John's College who maintained close ties with Annapolis, composed "The Star-Spangled Banner" while viewing the assault against the fort by the British ships.

In December 1824 General Lafayette, hero of the Revolution, returned to Annapolis and was treated to a festive weekend of balls, banquets, and tree plantings. In 1826 the Maryland Assembly began a campaign to promote Annapolis as the site of the long-proposed United States Naval School, but these proposals bore no fruit until the opening of the Naval Academy in October 1845. The navy was ceded old Fort Severn as the site for the Academy; the fort, later remodeled into a gymnasium, continued to dominate the entrance to Spa Creek until its demolition in 1909.

Probably the most colorful event that transpired in Annapolis during the mid-nineteenth century was the riot touched off by passengers from the steamship *Jewess*. On July 5, 1847, the steamship left Baltimore crowded with passengers headed for an excursion in St. Michaels. The ship was overloaded, however, and the captain, fearing for the safety of his passengers, finally put into Annapolis after a voyage of five hours. The disappointed pleasure seekers apparently ran amok in the town and were chased back to the ship by outraged Annapolitans. Just when Daniel Hyde, a prominent citizen of Annapolis, had persuaded the captain of *Jewess* to cast off, someone from the ship tossed a lemon at him. The citizens of Annapolis responded with a volley of bricks pried from the sidewalk; the Baltimoreans replied with pistols, and five Annapolitans fell wounded. The incensed crowd on shore seized the cannon from the old battery, loaded it, and trained it on the ship. They were prevented from firing only by Colonel George Kane, who flung his body across the muzzle of the gun. *Jewess* then made a fast getaway with no casualties.

At the outbreak of the Civil War the city's sympathies were solidly pro-Southern: Abraham Lincoln received only one vote in the election of 1860. After mobs attacked the Massachusetts Sixth Regiment in Baltimore in April 1861, the federal government ordered troops under the command of General Benjamin F. Butler to secure Annapolis for the safe passage of further Northern reinforcements. Although Governor Thomas H. Hicks favored remaining in the Union, the Democratic legislature did not; after the Battle of Bull Run, according to historian Donald Dozer, the entire legislature was arrested and interned in Northern prisons until the members swore an oath of loyalty to the Union. As the Southern states seceded from the Union, Southern midshipmen withdrew from the Naval Academy and headed home. In May 1861 the government loaded the remaining midshipmen on the USS *Constitution* and moved the Academy to Newport, Rhode Island, for the remainder of the war. The Academy was converted into a hospital for the treatment of the wounded, and St. John's College was transformed into a camp to house exchanged Union prisoners until the completion of the larger camp at Parole.

Throughout the war Annapolis was treated as an occupied city. When General Jubal Early invaded Maryland in July 1864, Annapolitans were impressed into digging a redoubt that extended the entire length of the Annapolis and Elkridge Railroad line, which ran along College Avenue and out West Street to Parole. The state government manumitted the slaves of Maryland on November 1, 1864, and the five hundred slaves living in Annapolis were among those affected by the long-awaited freedom. With Lee's surrender at Appomattox in 1865 Annapolitans breathed a sigh of relief; the single desire of the residents was to return to prewar normality.

Many changes came to Annapolis in the mid to late nineteenth century. The Annapolis and Elkridge Railroad, with its station on West Street, began operations on Christmas Day 1840. It was joined by the Shortline, with a station on Bladen Street, in 1887. In the 1870s a burst of prosperity led to the development of Conduit, Cathedral, and Franklin Streets. New houses were erected in the garden areas that had been the pride of eighteenth-century Annapolis, and the city attained its present urban character by 1900. Physical improvements to the streetscape accompanied this building boom. Although Annapolitans had begun to pave their sidewalks with brick in the 1820s, the streets remained muddy morasses until 1896–97, when the city council authorized the installation of "Belgian blocks" (stone paving blocks) on Main Street at a cost of $7,556. The paving of the other streets followed rapidly. The same decade saw the installation of the city water system, which replaced the common wells that previously stood on every street. Public hygiene improved markedly as baths were no longer limited to "once a week." Electrical service also began in the 1890s, and telephone service was established in 1899.

The Spanish-American War touched Annapolis in an unusual way. After the defeat of the Spanish fleet at Santiago in 1898, Admiral Cervera and his officers were sent to Annapolis to await repatriation. On July 16, 1898, seventy-nine elegant gentlemen of the Spanish Navy disembarked at the Naval Academy dock. The young American officer in charge of their paroles was somewhat concerned when one of the officers refused to sign promptly. Those who signed were at liberty to mingle with the townspeople, and they enjoyed much hospitality and attention, especially from the ladies. The last recalcitrant officer soon relented and joined in the gaiety. At least one romance was nipped in the bud when the young officer's mother wrote from Spain demanding that her son be sent home immediately before any indiscretion could take place.

Although the Spaniards departed in September, their visit was long remembered. They left one lone captive behind: a one-eyed parrot named Cristobal Colon. Despite his surly temper—he bit and clawed all who came within range—Cristobal became the unofficial mascot of the Naval Academy until his death in 1908. His passing was noted in the *New York Herald.*

The history of Annapolis in the twentieth century is the story of the growth of the state and local governments and the rise of the movement to preserve the city's colonial heritage. Between 1902 and 1905 the size of the State House was greatly expanded by an addition to the northwest side. A new neoclassical structure to house the Court of Appeals was erected across State Circle during the same years. Beginning with the James Building in 1939, the state erected a series of office buildings that eventually covered the entire tract between College Avenue and College Creek: the Treasury Building (1958), the State Income Tax Building (1967), the Lowe House of Delegates Office Building (1974), and the Legislative Services Building (1976). This last was erected on the site of the Court of Appeals Building, which was demolished in 1973 when the court moved to a new complex across College Creek on Rowe Boulevard. Although the architecture of the state office buildings is a generally sensitive rendition of Georgian Revival, their scale is overwhelming, and the massing of offices has made this once-thriving section of the city a ghost town after dark. The county government enlarged the courthouse on Church Circle several times, most recently in the 1990s. Arundel Center and a parking garage on Calvert Street were added in the 1960s. The annexation of Eastport, Wardour, Parole, and several other jurisdictions in 1951 nearly doubled the city's size and brought with it an accompanying expansion of municipal government. Aside from altering the city streetscape, this governmental expansion has had a profound effect on the economy of Annapolis. In 1976 the federal, state, county, and city governments employed approximately half of all people employed in the city. On the darker side, the property owned by the four levels of government as well as churches and schools now constitutes 45 percent of the value of all property in Annapolis. Since these properties are tax exempt, the city has been deprived of a potentially valuable source of income. The growth in public sector employment has been matched by a sharp decrease in the agriculture and fishery related jobs that formed the backbone of the city's economy in the nineteenth century. The sleepy market town has again become a major center of government.

Interest in preserving the historic buildings of Annapolis began in the 1880s under the leadership of Frank Mayer and his Local Improvement Society, a movement inspired in part by the state's insensitive modernization of the State House. Mayer and his group recognized that the rapid deterioration of the Annapolis economy had left the city with a priceless treasure: too poor to rebuild, Annapolitans had unconsciously inherited and preserved an almost intact eighteenth-century city.

Preservation efforts stepped up in the 1920s. St. John's College bought the Hammond-Harwood House in 1926 after hearing that Henry Ford had plans to carry off the house for reassembly at his outdoor museum at Greenfield Village in Michigan. The college hired R. T. H. Halsey in 1928 to create a decorative arts program using the Hammond-Harwood House and the Brice House to showcase a collection of antique Maryland furniture. The Depression, however, put a premature end to Halsey's scheme. The Brice House was divided into faculty apartments, and the Hammond-Harwood House was sold. The furnishings were returned to their owners, among them the Garvan family, early collectors of fine American furniture.

The 1930s were marked by more battles on the preservation front. The Hammond-Harwood House Association was formed in 1940. John D. Rockefeller originally had his eye on Annapolis when his interests turned to preservation, but the opposition of the Chamber of Commerce (which feared restrictive zoning) scared the philanthropist south to Williamsburg. A third preservation group, the Company for the Preservation of Colonial Annapolis, was chartered in 1925, but the company fell apart in the face of President Roosevelt's World War II plan to expand the Naval Academy to Prince George Street, annexing St. John's College and leveling everything on the tract. Fortunately, local opposition and the timely end of the war prevented the scheme from being implemented.

The most successful of the various preservation groups that have been organized in the city, Historic Annapolis, Inc., was founded in 1952. Intensive efforts by Historic Annapolis led to the designation of the downtown area as a registered National Historic Landmark District in 1966. Three years later the group persuaded the Annapolis City Council to put the historic district ordinance to a referendum, and the voters accepted the ordinance by a margin of two to one, thus providing the historic district of Annapolis with legal protection against modern encroachment. Historic Annapolis has also been active on a number of other fronts. It saved the Paca House from demolition in 1966 and subsequently restored the house and its eighteenth-century garden. The organization also runs several other enterprises, notably the Tobacco Prise and the Victualling Warehouse, site of their museum store. These projects have been complemented by the initiatives of individuals and other groups. Although specific measures advocated by Historic Annapolis have sometimes been controversial, the group has made Annapolitans aware of their heritage and demonstrated the value of preservation to the city's economy. The resurgence of small retailers on Main Street and at Market Space in the 1970s is in large part a measure of the success of preservation, making Annapolis a city attractive to sightseers and history buffs from across the nation.

In the over three and a half centuries since Thomas Todd settled on Spa Creek, Annapolis has seen many changes. It has developed from a port and colonial capital in the eighteenth century to a provincial market town in the nineteenth and finally to a governmental center and tourist attraction. But more than most cities, Annapolis has been able to preserve the record of its history in its institutions, its architecture, and its streetscape. This guidebook will enable the reader to trace at least a part of that record by walking the streets of Annapolis today.

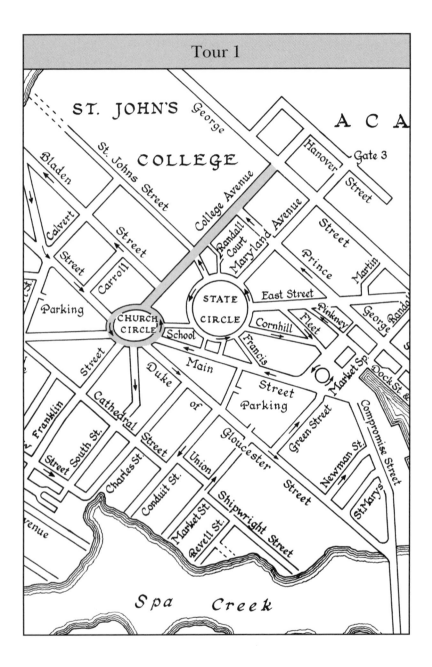

Tour 1

# Church Circle, College Avenue, and the St. John's College Campus

## *CHURCH CIRCLE*

### St. Anne's Episcopal Church

The conformation of Church Circle is the same today as it was in 1696 when Governor Nicholson laid out his baroque plan. Richard Beard had previously made the first plat (or "plot") of the town, and he superimposed Nicholson's plan over his own original plot.

The appearance of *St. Anne's Episcopal Church* has changed dramatically from the original building, which was begun in 1695 and stood till 1774. This first building, the church of Middle Neck Parish, was finished in 1704. The architect, probably Thomas Fielder, stipulated that a gold ball was to be placed on the top of the steeple, and that is the only feature of the building that is documented today. The communion service arrived in 1696 as a gift from King William III, and it is still in use. It was made by Francis Garthorne, court silversmith, in 1695, and it bears King William's coat of arms.

St. Anne's Episcopal Church had high wooden pews, owned by such families as the Pacas, the Chases, and the Carrolls, and also by Governors Charles and Leonard Calvert. The churchyard contains many early graves, but by 1790 the church had to acquire additional land for burials.

By 1774 the original building was much too small to accommodate the parishioners, who were required by law to attend the established church. The church was dismantled and materials were gathered to build a new one. The Revolutionary War

intervened, however, and the new building was not ready for occupancy until seventeen years later. Between the demolition of the old church and the construction of the new, the congregation met in the theater on West Street and in King William's School.

Disaster struck St. Anne's in 1858 when a fire destroyed the building. Fortunately, the records, communion service, and Bible were saved. The only portions of the building left standing were the bell tower, the doorway, and the front wall, and these features were incorporated into the new church, built in the Lombard Romanesque Revival style and sufficiently finished to be used for services by July 1859. In 1866 the town installed a new bell in the recently completed tower; the bell was first rung on Christmas Eve of that year. The town clock is also in the tower.

The graves of early leaders of the town lie in the circle around the church. Sir Robert Eden, the last colonial governor of Maryland, is buried there. The oldest original grave, that of Amos Garrett, the first mayor of Annapolis, is dated 1727. Several older gravestones from neighboring parishes have been moved to St. Anne's for preservation, including the stones of Nicholas Greenbury (one of those appointed by Governor Nicholson to lay out the town in 1694, dated 1697); his wife Anne (1698); and Major John Hammond (the grandfather of Mathias Hammond, 1707). It was Major John Hammond who made the bequest to the church for the purchase of the large Bible, now called the Hammond Bible, which is still owned by St. Anne's.

One of the most colorful figures associated with St. Anne's during its long history was Joseph Simmons, who served as sexton of the church for nearly seventy years until his death in 1836 at the age of one hundred. Simmons was popularly known as Joe Morgue due to his long monopoly on that traditional sideline of

St. Anne's Episcopal Church, Church Circle

sextons, grave digging. An almost Dickensian character, Joe Morgue roamed the streets of Annapolis, his hair long and unkempt and his clothing outmoded. When taunted by schoolchildren for his eccentric appearance, his standard retort was, "I'll have *you* someday."

One of the most celebrated anecdotes about Joe Morgue concerned his behavior at the funeral of Jeffrey Jig, an unusual person who periodically fell into a comatose state and was several times prepared for burial before reviving. On one such occasion Jig had already been placed in the grave when a furious knocking was heard from the coffin. Joe Morgue continued to hurl earth into the grave. When entreated by Jig's family to desist, he responded, "He's got to die sometime; and if he's not dead, he ought to be." The mourners eventually did succeed in restraining the sexton, and Jeffrey Jig survived to die another day.

## Around Church Circle from Northwest Street

*3 Church Circle* is a late nineteenth-century office building remodeled in the twentieth-century commercial style with Italianate detail. It has always been used for commercial purposes.

*4 Church Circle* is of the same period but in the Tudor Revival style. It is also used for commercial purposes.

*5 Church Circle, Farmers National Bank,* was built in 1812 as a hyphen and octagonal wing connected to Reynolds Tavern, which housed the bank's cashier. Originally one story in height, the wing has repeatedly been remodeled and enlarged. Traces of the octagonal plan and some early brickwork are still visible on the Church Circle facade.

*7 Church Circle, Reynolds Tavern,* was built about 1747 on land set aside for the support and maintenance of the rector of St. Anne's. The site was leased by the church to William Reynolds for

Reynolds Tavern, Church Circle

a tavern in 1747. In 1764 Robert Reynolds advertised that he made hats of the best "furrs" at his father's shop "over against St. Anne's in Annapolis." In the 1760s William Reynolds also ran a stocking factory adjacent to the tavern, producing, among other things, stockings that had the word "AMERICA" running down the leg. The building later served as the home of the cashier of the Farmers National Bank and in 1936 became the Annapolis Public Library. Archaeological excavations undertaken by a team from the University of Maryland in 1982 uncovered a wealth of early eighteenth-century artifacts. Now restored, the building is used for the entertainment of twenty-first-century visitors to Annapolis.

*6 Church Circle, Circuit Court for Anne Arundel County* (commonly called *Anne Arundel County Courthouse),* was built in the Federal style in 1821–24. The central projecting porch and tower were added in 1892. Further expansion occurred in 1923 and again in 1929. A large Colonial Revival wing was added between 1949 and 1952. In 1997 that addition was removed to make room for a new, massive 240,000-square-foot addition, which fills the entire block between South and Franklin Streets.

*10 Church Circle, Bank of America,* occupies the long lot between South and Duke of Gloucester Streets. Built in 1972, its brick construction, pedestrian arcade, and low height (two stories with mansard roof) represent an attempt to construct a building that would harmonize with the neighboring eighteenth- and nineteenth-century structures on Church Circle. The attempt does not quite succeed—the horizontal emphasis of the façade exaggerates the building's mass—but the architecture of the bank was an attempt at compatible twentieth-century design in the Historic District.

*16 Church Circle, The Maryland Inn,* was built in the 1770s on land originally set aside as "the Drummer's Lot." The drummer was the Annapolis town crier. The inn is a Georgian building with Victorian additions. The original structure was built by Thomas Hyde, who advertised it in the *Maryland Gazette* in 1782 as "An elegant brick house adjoining Church Circle in a dry and healthy part of the city, 100 feet front, 3 story high, 22 rooms, 20 fireplaces, 2 kitchens. Rooms mostly large and well furnished, and is one of the first houses in the State built as a house of entertainment, for which purpose it was originally intended." Fine porches, painted in vivid nineteenth-century colors, hug the sides of this flatiron-shaped building.

*The Annapolis Bank and Trust Company,* founded in 1904, occupies the site of a nineteenth-century hostelry known as Kaiser's Hotel. Some of the hotel seems to have been incorporated into the present structure. The small scale and fine detail of this building provide a good foil to the Maryland Inn on the other side of Main Street.

On the northeast corner of Church Circle is *Southgate Cross* with its fountain. It was erected in 1901 by the citizens of Annapolis in memory of Dr. William Southgate, who served as rector of St. Anne's longer than any other man, from 1869 to 1899. The fountain basin served as a watering trough for horses until World War II.

*The Post Office,* built in 1901 in the Georgian Revival style, boasts elaborate carved paneling on the interior. Noteworthy features such as the Palladian windows, the stone swags applied to the walls, and the soaring cupola are based on well-known historic buildings in Maryland, Virginia, and England.

## COLLEGE AVENUE

This street, which runs in front of St. John's College, was originally called Back Street. In the eighteenth century the name was changed to Tabernacle Street, and in the nineteenth century to College Avenue. The block from King George Street to the Naval Academy wall was sold in the late nineteenth century to freed black townspeople who built small row houses.

## From the Naval Academy to Church Circle

*11 College Avenue* was built about 1800 in the Federal style as a town house, typical of the period in Annapolis.

*15–17–19 College Avenue* make up a row of buildings built in the Victorian style as residences about 1880.

*22–24–26 College Avenue* form another row of identical buildings built about 1885 as residences.

*29–31 College Avenue* is a double house with a Greek Revival temple front. The house has Italianate eaves, and a bull's-eye window adorns the pediment on the College Avenue facade.

*Ogle Hall,* at the corner of College Avenue and King George Street, was constructed by Dr. William Stevenson and completed shortly before his death in 1739. The house was then occupied by his widow Francina and her new husband, Daniel Cheston.

In 1747 the house was rented to Governor Samuel Ogle and his wife, Anne Tasker Ogle. The Ogle family's country estate in Prince George's County was Belair, where they kept an extensive stable of thoroughbred racing stock. Ogle Hall served as the Governor's Mansion when the Ogles were in residence. In 1753 Daniel Cheston sold the house to Colonel Benjamin Tasker for seventy tons of Tasker's Baltimore pig iron. Tasker then resold it to his sister, Anne Tasker Ogle, by that time a widow. In the course of time, Anne Tasker Ogle sold the house to her son Benjamin, who became governor of Maryland in 1798. Benjamin Ogle and his wife Henrietta, nicknamed Henry, added a semi-octagonal ballroom to the rear of the mansion in 1776. During the Revolution, Henry Ogle wrote to her mother-in-law, Anne Ogle, expressing fear that the British would bombard the town: "It would be horrid provoking to have our House beat down

Ogle Hall, corner of College Avenue and King George Street

now we have almost finished it." The Ogles continued to hold the house until 1815, when it was quite safe from British shells. General Lafayette visited Ogle Hall in 1824.

The Porter family bought the house in 1867. Vice Admiral David Dixon Porter was superintendent of the Naval Academy during the period of rebuilding after the Civil War. He also introduced a new curriculum that stressed the study of engineering. In 1945 the Naval Academy Alumni Association bought the house and restored it, largely through the efforts of Harry England, to its original elegance. It has served as an alumni visitors' center since that time.

The building is of brick, laid in Flemish bond, with a twentieth-century entrance on King George Street. In the eighteenth century, visitors entered through the College Avenue door into the hallway. They could enjoy the garden by going out the jib door, the center bay on the King George Street front of the building.

*61 College Avenue* is a great town house built in 1881 by Commodore James Iredell Waddell, the captain of the CSS *Shenandoah.* Commodore Waddell took command of his Liverpool-built steamer in the Madeira Islands and set sail to capture and destroy Union shipping. After terrorizing ships along the African Coast, he sailed south and east past the Cape of Good Hope and on eastward through the Indian Ocean to Australia. From there, he headed north into the Bering Sea where he found the New Bedford whaling fleet, the Union shipping especially targeted by this cruise. The captains of those ships tried to convince Commodore Waddell that the war was over, but to no avail. He disabled or sank twenty-one ships. He then sailed to San Francisco where a newspaper report persuaded him that the war was, indeed, over. He hastily sailed for England where he stayed for two years. Then he returned to Annapolis with his wife who was an Annapolis native.

The brick house that the Waddells built and occupied for many years is a rare example of the British-inspired Queen Anne style, not unlike houses erected in Liverpool at that time. Gossips said that the money to build this large, impressive building came from the booty Waddell had amassed on the long voyage of the CSS *Shenandoah.* The massive concrete porch on the College Avenue front of the house is especially noteworthy.

## ST. JOHN'S COLLEGE CAMPUS

*St. John's College* today covers thirty-two acres, bounded by King George Street, St. John's Street, College Avenue, and College Creek. The college traces its beginnings from King William's School, established in 1696. In 1784 the college was chartered to serve as the western shore branch of the proposed University of Maryland, and the two schools were consolidated into one in 1786. Among the early students at St. John's were two nephews of George Washington, and also Francis Scott Key, who wrote "The Star-Spangled Banner." All three graduated in 1796. The college became a military school in 1884, then became a liberal arts college in 1923, and adopted the Great Books program of liberal arts education in 1937. In 1951 the college became coeducational. It opened a second campus in Santa Fe, New Mexico, in 1964.

*The Greensward* on which the campus is located has had a long history of public use in Annapolis. The area along College Creek was at one time the town pasture.

The *Liberty Tree,* once a historic landmark, was a large tulip poplar estimated to be four hundred years old. Under this tree's branches the Sons of Liberty met to discuss separation from England before the Revolution, deeming it wiser to gather in the open where all comers could be observed rather than to meet furtively indoors. The Marquis de Lafayette reviewed the Maryland Militia under the tree in 1824 when he made his sentimental American visit. Commencement exercises at St. John's were held under its branches for many years.

On September 16, 1999, Hurricane Floyd struck Annapolis with great force. Thousands of trees were downed or damaged, including the Liberty Tree. The tree had weathered other adversities but after four hundred years this insult was the last it could handle. After much consultation with various tree experts it was regretfully decided to remove the tree, and it was taken down on October 25, 1999. Some of the wood was salvaged and used to make musical instruments and other presentation pieces. A plaque may be placed on the spot where the tree stood for so many years.

The oldest building on the campus, the *Carroll House* was origi-nally located at the corner of Main and Conduit Streets. Built in 1722 by Dr. Charles Carroll, the Chirurgeon (surgeon), it was the birthplace of Charles Carroll, the Barrister, author of the Maryland Bill of Rights. These two Carrolls are believed to be distant Protestant cousins of the better known Catholic Carrolls. The Carroll House passed through several owners until 1955 when it was destined for demolition so that the valuable com-mercial site it occupied could be developed. The owner offered the house to Historic Annapolis if it could be moved, and moved it was, over six blocks of city streets entwined with utility wires and crowded with gaping spectators. The house was exten-sively restored and is used today as the admissions office of St. John's College.

Another old building on the campus is the *Chancellor Johnson House,* located on St. John's Street. It was moved to its present location in 1937, also for reasons of preservation. The small eighteenth-century frame building originally stood a block away on Northwest Street and at one time was an "ordinary," or tavern.

The central building on the St. John's campus is *McDowell Hall.* In 1744 Governor Thomas Bladen began construction of a building intended for use as his Governor's Mansion. The plan was grand, and after Bladen made further applications for money, the legislature decided it was clearly extravagant and cut off funds. The house was left without a roof, windows, or doors,

McDowell Hall, St. John's College Campus, College Avenue

and was soon called Bladen's Folly. Thomas Jefferson, however, felt it had promise. In 1766 he visited Annapolis and noted, "They have no publick building worth mentioning except a governor's house, the hall of which after being finished, they have suffered to go to ruin." The design is what Jefferson praised, and the Scot Simon Duff is credited as the architect. His "undertaker," or contractor, was Patrick Creagh.

By 1784 St. John's College, chartered from the assets of King William's School, was in need of a site and the legislature deeded it Bladen's Folly. It took five more years for the college to complete two classrooms; by the late 1790s the building was finally complete. Fifty years had elapsed from groundbreaking to completion.

McDowell Hall, named for St. John's first president, John McDowell, originally housed students and classrooms. The hall served as a ballroom when Lafayette visited Annapolis in 1824. Although used as a Union prison during the Civil War and gutted by fire twice, McDowell Hall was partially restored to its original plan and renovated in 1989. It now houses the office of the president of the college. The Seneca sandstone porch on the east front, salvaged from the 1886 State House library annex, was added in 1903 at a cost of $520.

Among the treasures of St. John's is "Dr. Bray's Library." In 1699 Princess Anne directed that 1,058 volumes of classics, new scientific works, and literature of the day be sent to Bray, the don of King William's School, to aid him in educating his students. The library, the largest collection of books in the colonies at that time, is now housed in the Maryland State Archives.

The campus boasts a number of other buildings of architectural merit, including several early examples of nineteenth-century Gothic Revival. Visitors are welcome to stroll through the campus to savor its sense of history.

# West Street, Franklin Street, Acton Place, and Parole

## *WEST STREET*

Near the southwest corner of West Street and Church Circle is the site of the *Crown and Dial Tavern* (see 31–33 West Street) which was run by William Faris, an Annapolis silversmith and watchmaker. The tavern, garden, and shop were on the south side of West Street and extended all the way to Cathedral. Faris was born in England in 1728. His father, a clockmaker, died when William was an infant, and his mother moved to Philadelphia. By 1757 Faris had resettled in Annapolis, married a local girl, Priscilla Woodward, and set himself up as a silversmith as well as a tavern keeper. The Farises had nine children. Faris leased the Crown and Dial at first but eventually purchased it in the late 1750s. It was soon enlarged to accommodate a growing family and business. William Faris, an avid gardener, was very partial to holly trees. A vestryman at St. Anne's, Faris was generally mild-mannered and pious, but he kept up a running feud with Abram Claude, a clockmaker who kept shop across the street. Faris's sons all went to sea, except for one who could not get along with his father. Between 1792 and 1804 Faris kept a diary that remains one of the best accounts of Annapolis life in the eighteenth century. On the death of William Faris in 1804, the business was taken over by his wife Priscilla and an apprentice.

Silver pieces made by Faris were owned by Samuel Chase, Charles Carroll of Carrollton, and Walter Dulany. Faris maintained and wound clocks for William Paca and Thomas Jennings.

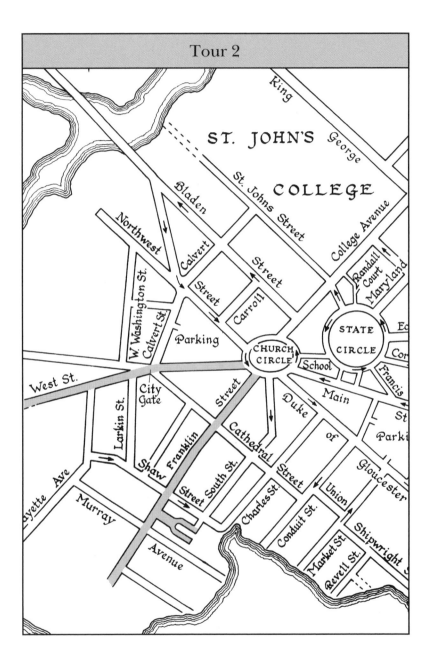

Tour 2

William Buckland recorded stopping at the tavern for "sangree" or an occasional "todey," both specialties of the eighteenth-century barkeep's art.

Close by the location of Faris's tavern was the theater where the congregation of St. Anne's Church met for services during the seventeen-year period when the second church was under construction. Although the first church had been razed in 1775, construction lapsed during the Revolution and was not resumed until 1785. The new church was consecrated in 1792.

The area from the City Gate (at the corner of Cathedral and West Streets) to Church Circle developed early as a center for craftsmen and tavern keepers. As the years passed, banks and businesses have located in the block, but it still retains some of the flavor of the past, thanks in large part to the Historic Preservation Commission.

## From Church Circle to Cathedral and Calvert Streets

*18 West Street* was built in the 1780s by Allen Quynn. It is an outstanding example of Federal architecture. The granite steps and the floor length windows and grilles are products of a pre–Civil War remodeling. The interior paneling and other woodwork, especially the interior shutters, add to the architectural value of the structure. It now serves as a professional office building.

*26–28 West Street* is a Georgian-style building which retains many of its eighteenth-century details. The brickwork is a mixture of English and header bond, and the structure retains the original dormers in the attic and massive end chimneys. The building has been handsomely restored and serves as the Annapolis Anne Arundel Conference and Visitors' Bureau. The entrance is on the side of the building with parking accessed from the Northwest Street side.

*30 West Street* is a pre-Revolutionary building that lost much of its integrity with the addition of the storefront. The second floor is intact and the chimneys and dormers are original.

*31–33 West Street* was William Faris's *Crown and Dial Tavern*. The building retains much of its eighteenth-century character, with massive end chimneys, triangular attic dormer, and most of the windows intact. Number 31 possesses a nineteenth-century doorway.

*45–50 West Street* was built about 1750 by Charles Carroll and was used as a tavern. The first two stories of the building have been altered, but the attic dormers are the original ones. The storefront has changed the appearance of the ground level.

## *FRANKLIN STREET*

Franklin Street corresponds approximately to the location of Doctor's Street according to the 1718 Stoddert survey of Annapolis. This area originally belonged to the vestry of St. Anne's but portions were leased for many purposes. Thomas Hyde operated a tanyard (yard for tanning hides) on the site of the present County Courthouse throughout the eighteenth century. The buildings along the street were mostly residential until the requirements of both the Anne Arundel Medical Center and the County Courthouse prompted their conversion to office space.

## From Church Circle to Spa Creek

*92–94 Franklin Street,* the *Wells-Ridout* double house, was built around 1840 in the Federal style. Its most interesting feature is the covered alleyway that separates the two halves of the building. Number 94 was first owned by Dr. John B. Wells and later by Edward Thompson. Wells, a former surgeon in the United States Army, was the uncle of George Wells, the Clerk of the Circuit Court. Number 92 Franklin Street may have been built by John Shaw, a relative of John Shaw the cabinetmaker. In 1818 Shaw sold the lot for number 92 to Samuel Ridout, a lawyer and mayor of Annapolis. Dr. John Ridout, son of Samuel, sold the property to Jane D. McElheney. After her ownership it passed back into the hands of St. Anne's Episcopal Church and was long used as a home for the sexton. Today number 92 is used as a law office, and number 94 is occupied by county offices.

*84 Franklin Street* was Mount Moriah A.M.E. Church, which began as an organized church in 1799. It was actually chartered in 1803 and became affiliated with the African Methodist Episcopal Church in 1816. The present building was erected in 1876 in the neo-Gothic style. Following severe storm damage in 1896 it was remodeled in 1897 as Victorian Gothic.

The interior woodwork was honey oak, and the stained glass windows were beautifully colored. When the congregation built a new church, the building was deeded to Anne Arundel County, which in 1972 decided to demolish it after selling off the windows and the interior furnishings at auction. Legal action by the city government in 1974 thwarted the destruction of this landmark. The building is now the *Banneker-Douglass Museum,* a museum of African-American history and culture.

*67–69 Franklin Street* is a tall, elegant, Italianate brick building. Constructed in 1876 by George Franklin, who owned it for many years, the double building is now used for offices.

*63–65 Franklin Street* another double house, was built in the shingle style by Joseph R. Wilmer in 1904. Wilmer operated a boys' preparatory school here. Homes such as this one are reminiscent of Newport and other New England resort towns.

*61 Franklin Street* was built in 1903, also in the shingle style. It reflects the Dutch Colonial Revival popular in the early twentieth century. The house features a gambrel roof and massive chimney facing the street.

The southeast corner of Franklin and Cathedral Streets was long the site of Anne Arundel General Hospital. The site was originally owned by Edwin A. Seidowitz, a florist. At the time of the Revolution, the site was owned by Major Richard Tootell, a physician who maintained a "Medical Shop" there. He also made his home there, a structure later described as a "dwelling . . . of a colonial structure and small."

The Annapolis Emergency Hospital Association was founded in 1902 and the original hospital consisted of eleven beds. The community soon outgrew the small hospital and a larger building was constructed in 1910 after a successful fund-raising campaign. It was damaged by fire in 1927 and repaired. In the mid-twentieth century, with continued growth, the hospital became Anne Arundel General Hospital, and in the early 1990s, Anne Arundel Medical Center. The hospital relocated in 2002. Plans for the site of the original hospital include development, possibly called Acton's Landing, for mixed residential use.

## *ACTON PLACE*

### Off Franklin Street,
### Between Shaw Street and Murray Avenue

*1 Acton Place.* Although its location was once outside the confines of the city limits, Acton is too significant to be missed. The land on which the present building stands was granted to Richard Acton by Cecil Calvert in 1651. The Georgian-style house was begun in 1772 by John Hammond (brother of Matthias, who built Hammond-Harwood House) and his wife, the daughter of John Brice. The central section of the house consists of five bays—two temple fronts with a central recessed bay unlike the typical Georgian house. Two massive chimneys face the street and soar above the temple fronts. A distinctive window dominates the late nineteenth-century front porch. This double-front design is quite sophisticated for the early date of the house. The rear of Acton is equally interesting. A demioctagonal bay projects from the center of the back wall, and a jib door gives access to the garden. A one-story porch, also octagonal in design, wraps around the bay. The brick of Acton, a unique carmine red in color, is laid in Flemish bond. A hyphen and wing were added to the south side of Acton in 1910 and are slightly out of scale with the main block.

Recently, the grounds and building of Acton have been significantly refurbished. The sensitive restoration work still manages to incorporate modern features, for example, the solar collector on the east side of the north wing. Acton is best seen from the head of Acton Place. Although the grounds are not open to the public, the visitor can obtain a good view of the garden from the cul-de-sac on the north side of the house and from the water.

## PAROLE

### West Street, Between Chinquapin Round Road and Old Solomon's Island Road

Although Parole is not within walking distance of the historic district, it is included here because of its historical connection to early Annapolis. Horseracing, "the sport of kings," was much favored by the colonists in Maryland. As early as the 1740s Annapolis had a formal racecourse, carefully laid out in the area just beyond the City Gate at the intersection of West and Cathedral Streets. The course was subsequently moved to a site farther out West Street in present-day Parole.

Samuel Ogle's permanent residence was in Prince George's County at Belair, where he had a large stable of racehorses. Some of his stock was imported from England. When he was

appointed colonial governor in 1747, Ogle and his wife Anne
Tasker Ogle rented the house at the corner of King George
Street and College Avenue. The building would later be named
for the family (see tour 1, Ogle Hall). Ogle's great interest in
racing led him to form the Jockey Club and to spearhead the installation of a regulation three-mile racecourse, possibly the first
in America. Gentlemen had traditionally spurred their horses
along the road now called West Street from the City Gate to
Three Mile Oak. The huge old oak stood at the end of the
course, where Routes 178 (General's Highway) and 450 (Defense Highway) meet today. It was felled by lightning in the
1960s, but a historic marker was placed in the general area
about two blocks to the east.

In 1767 the Jockey Club met at the Maryland Coffee House,
located at 199 Church (Main) Street and run by John Ball.
George Washington noted in his diary that he attended a meeting there and that dinner followed. In 1770 the Jockey Club met
at Middleton's Tavern on the Dock, where the announcement
was made of a meeting to be held on "Tuesday, 4 June 1770."
Governor Eden and Horatio Sharpe, Esq., were "Stewards." Dinner was to be served at two o'clock, and those proposing to attend were requested to send notice to William Eddis, secretary.

George Washington set out on September 21, 1771, "with
Mr. Wormley for the Annapolis races." He doesn't remark on
how his horse did on the meeting day. The course "drew sport-
ing gentry from far and wide in colonial days." Behind the race-
track was a famous fountain, described as a "boiling spring that
welled up from deep in the earth and bubbled through a heavy
layer of clean sand, which gave it a shimmering appearance.
The clear, cold water was drunk or dipped from the surface, and
was pure and sweet." In the 1960s "a soft drink company brought
tank trucks to the spring and drew its entire water supply from
it." Consequently, Annapolis missed out on the mineral water
boom of the 1970s and the opportunity to bottle a domestic
Perrier was lost.

*Parole* is so called because it was the site of Camp Parole, a Union camp established in November 1861. It was first the site of a squatters' camp of the Fifty-third New York Infantry, the Zouaves. The function of the camp changed when Union deserters were sent there rather than to St. John's campus, the previous site of the stockade. They frightened the citizens when they wandered about so the camp was moved out of town. Seventy thousand prisoners were processed through Camp Parole. After the Civil War, former slaves and their families settled on the campsite and many of their descendants still own land in the area.

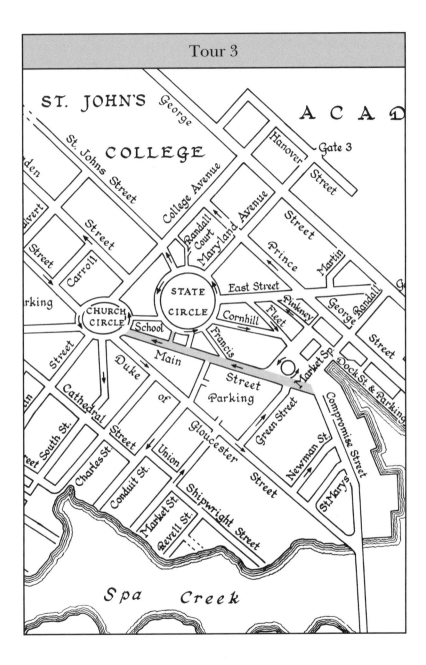

# Main Street

## MAIN STREET

Until the beginning of the twentieth century Main Street was known as Church Street; a street sign bearing the older name can still be seen affixed to the facade of 206 Main Street. The area where Main Street merges with Compromise Street had long been the warehouse district of Annapolis. Warehouses owned by various businessmen held imported goods as well as tobacco and other produce to be shipped to England. The wharves ran out into the cove for easy loading and unloading. By 1765 there was even a tavern in the area called the "Sign of the White Hart." In 1790 a devastating fire destroyed the entire block. Rebuilding took about twenty years.

## Dock to Conduit Street

*77 Main Street,* "the Warehouse of the Victualling Office," as it was called during the Revolution, was confiscated from its Loyalist owner, Daniel Dulany of Walter, by the State of Maryland. It was used to store supplies awaiting shipment to the Continental Army. By 1816, George and John Barber's large dry-goods store occupied the site. The Barbers ran steam packets from their wharf. The nineteenth-century building on the site has been restored to reflect the long tradition of warehouses in the area. It is still owned by the State of Maryland.

*81–83 Main Street,* the site of the White Hart Tavern, is a Federal-style building where Jacob Slemaker made hats. The building is unchanged except for the storefront.

*99 Main Street* was built by Frederick Grammar in 1792–98 strictly as a rental property. Grammar became wealthy baking bread for the Continental Army in his shop at the "head of Duke of Gloucester Street" (see tour 4, 179 Duke of Gloucester Street). He rented the building to Lewis Neth, who lived upstairs and sold imported goods such as fabrics, stationery supplies, and even groceries. Neth's lease extended until his death. By the 1950s the building had led such a checkered life that it was threatened with demolition. It was purchased in 1958 by Port of Annapolis, Inc., a private consortium that restored it and sold it to Historic Annapolis. The building is a fine example of Georgian architecture, with Flemish bond brickwork, handsome wooden cornice with modillions, and two large chimneys.

*100 Main Street* is the *Goodman Building,* erected about 1900 in the "modern classical" style to house Aaron Goodman's commercial emporium. The building is now shared by a number of small businesses.

*101–107 Main Street* was originally two brick buildings constructed between 1816 and 1820 with shops on the ground floor and living space above.

*113–115 Main Street* was built about 1819–21 with three floors and a mansard roof that was added in the nineteenth century. Many of the stores and shops on Main Street are housed in eighteenth-century buildings that have been changed only by the opening of the storefront windows.

*132–134 Main Street* is a late eighteenth-century Federal building erected about 1791 by the merchant Joseph Dowson. The property was sold to Dowson's tenant William Wilkens when Dowson defaulted on his mortgage. Wilkens had lost his original shop, which was located in the first block of Main Street, in the 1790 fire.

*141–145 Main Street* may have been built by the Annapolis silversmith John Chalmers in 1770. Along with property at 149–151, the buildings were altered in 1870 when the Italianate style was popular.

*155 Main Street* is at the corner of Main and Francis Streets. A late Georgian building, it was altered in 1913 to its present form. The site of a grocery store in the late nineteenth century and a clothing store in the twentieth century, it has also housed a bank.

## Conduit Street to Church Circle

The corner of Conduit and Main Street has always been busy. In the 1770s most of the block between Main and Duke of Gloucester Streets and from Conduit Street to Green Street was owned by Lloyd Dulany. On the opposite corner was the home of Dr. Charles Carroll, the Chirurgeon (surgeon). The house was built about 1723 and was long the Carroll family home. In 1955 it was moved to the St. John's campus, where it serves a useful purpose today as an administration building. Only the two largest sections of the house were moved (see tour 1, Carroll House).

*158–164 Main Street* originally constituted one building, modern appearances notwithstanding. This Federal structure once boasted double chimneys braced by massive walls at either end. The chimneys have now disappeared, but their capped stumps are still visible from the opposite side of Main Street. The classically decorated penthouse above number 162 is a twentieth-century addition.

*176 Main Street* is called the *Matthews-Shorter House*. It was built between 1834 and 1842 by Charles Shorter and was owned by Henry Matthews, a "free black" tradesman. The building was owned by blacks for sixty years.

*181–183 Main Street* is the section of the Dr. Carroll house that was not moved to St. John's campus.

*200 Main Street,* now the rear of the State House Inn, was once called the White Cross Tavern and then the Capital Hotel. On the north side of the building is Chancery Lane, a steep flight of steps that runs from Main Street to State Circle.

*206 Main Street* overlooks the other side of Chancery Lane. It is an 1840 Greek Revival structure, built for commercial purposes. The building is noteworthy for its fine brick pilasters and pedimented gable.

*211 Main Street* was built about 1820 by the city of Annapolis to serve as City Hall. It also housed the city's fire engine and for many years sported a rooftop belfry. After the city moved its offices to Duke of Gloucester Street in the 1870s, number 211 was converted to Worthington's Drug Store.

*230–236 Main Street* is called the *Price House,* built as two attached buildings between 1820 and 1841 by Henry Price, who was described as a "free person of color." He died in February of 1863 and was said to have been much loved by the people of the city. The Price House stands on the site of the saddlery and sign-painting shop operated by the painter Charles Willson Peale from 1763 to 1765.

# Duke of Gloucester, Cathedral, Charles, Conduit, Market, Shipwright, and Green Streets

## *DUKE OF GLOUCESTER STREET*

Duke of Gloucester Street, originally called Southeast Street, runs from St. Anne's Church to Spa Creek. It was named for the young Duke of Gloucester, the oldest surviving son of Queen Anne and her consort, Prince George of Denmark. The buildings along the street date from the early eighteenth century to the early twentieth century. The Drummer's Lot, the site of the Maryland Inn, is where the drummer, or town crier, beat his drum to announce the happenings in the village.

## From Church Circle to Compromise Street

*223–225 Duke of Gloucester Street* is a double house built in the early nineteenth century of brick in the Federal style. It possesses two stories plus a dormered third floor and a large central chimney. This house represents the style of buildings erected after the Revolution when the city's prosperity was on the decline. It was built very simply and neatly decorated on the exterior in sharp contrast to the magnificent mansions of twenty-five or thirty years earlier.

*211 Duke of Gloucester Street* is a Victorian residence, built in the mid-1800s of clapboard. The small row of brown-shingled houses in the rear was built shortly after the turn of the twentieth century.

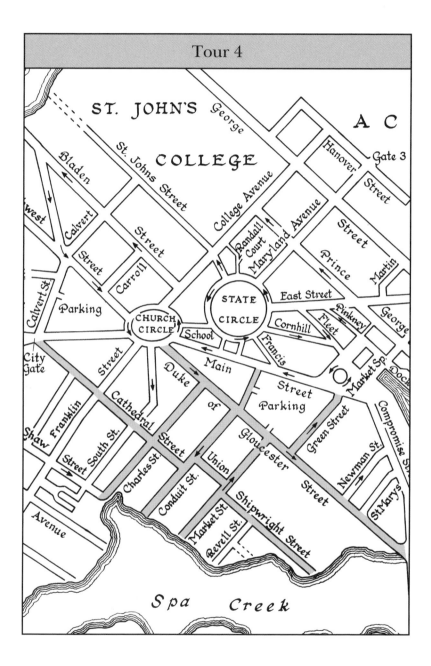

*199 Duke of Gloucester Street* is an early twentieth-century Colonial Revival structure, originally built as the rectory of St. Anne's and now used as the Parish House.

*195 Duke of Gloucester Street* is a late Second Empire house with a very fine mansard roof. An early building on this site was a tavern called the Lord Baltimore Arms.

*192 Duke of Gloucester Street,* called Hyde House after the builder Thomas Hyde, is a colonial building constructed as a residence. In Thomas Hyde's day it served as a residence and in 1776, he offered it for rent and described it as follows: "where I now live, suitable for a genteel family, a good well of water in the yard, and necessary outbuildings, garden etc." In 1777 the property was rented to the government for the Commissary of Stores, and so it was used for the duration of the Revolutionary War.

The property has also served the First Presbyterian Church of Annapolis as a manse, and in the nineteenth century it housed the Workingmen's Building and Loan Association. It is now an office building.

*184 Duke of Gloucester Street* was built in the 1860s by Daniel Sprogle, a carpenter and mason. The symmetrical five-bay facade reflects the enduring Georgian influence. However, the mid-nineteenth century Italianate features include the Venetian window at the heavy bracketed cornice, heavy window molds, and the stonelike stucco finish. The house befits a successful builder who had recently completed the First Presbyterian Church and who became one of the developers of Eastport.

*179 Duke of Gloucester Street* was built in 1774 for the John Griffith family. The Georgian-style residence has two stories with dormer windows plus a half-story light. The brick is laid in Flemish bond and decorated with a high water table, belt course, and large chimney. The house, originally five bays in length, was reduced by half its size about 1870 when Conduit Street was extended from Duke of Gloucester Street to Spa Creek; the southwest corner shows repaired mortar. Parts of the two bays that were demolished were apparently used in the construction of the kitchen wing that extends along Conduit Street.

On the death of John Griffith the house passed to his nephew, John Griffith Worthington, and was owned by that family through the Revolutionary War, after which time the interior of the house was probably finished. It stands out, even with the changes that have taken place over the years, as one of the outstanding Georgian-style houses in Annapolis.

During the Revolution, the bakery of Frederick Grammar was located somewhere in the first or second block of Duke of Gloucester Street. In 1790, for speculation, Grammar erected the building known as the Sign of the Whale on the dock. He rented his building to Lewis Neth, who kept a store there until his death.

*170 Duke of Gloucester Street* was built in 1747 as a single-bay two-story residence by Henry Woodward as a tenement or rental. In 1760 the Forensic Club met there. William Paca was a member of the club, which held bimonthly meetings that usually lasted for five hours and included dinner. The members debated both sides of such issues as "Whether the People have a Right to dethrone a King," and one that is still debated today—"Whether soldiers doubting the justice of a war ought to fight." Other members of the club were George Diggs, James Tilghman, Charles Willson Peale, and Samuel Chase. Samuel Chase was expelled after nine months of membership for his "extremely irregular and indecent behavior."

The front windows and brickwork reveal several periods of construction as the house was enlarged from three bays to five in the late eighteenth century. It became part of the City Hotel property when George Mann acquired it. He leased it to William Coe, a tailor. As part of his rent, Coe supplied clothing for the servants and slaves of the Mann family.

*The Municipal Building* at *164 Duke of Gloucester Street* is constructed on the site of the Annapolis Assembly Rooms, built in 1764. William Eddis described "apartments" at each end of the building with card tables set up for those who chose to game the evening away. The rooms were "illuminated with great brilliancy and balls were [held] fortnightly in winter." During the Revolution, however, the Assembly was discontinued. The city government moved to the Assembly Rooms in the 1870s after it outgrew the cramped quarters at 211 Main Street. The original building was destroyed by fire, but the new City Hall incorporates three walls of the old building, those facing west, north, and south. The Annapolis City Council meets on the second floor today; regular meetings are held the second Monday of each month.

*163 Duke of Gloucester Street,* the *Maynard-Burgess House,* was the home of two successive African-American families from 1847–1900. John Maynard, a free black, purchased the house in 1847 "with buildings." Architectural evidence indicates that it was at least in part a later eighteenth-century outbuilding, which he expanded to its present form. Maynard was a waiter, possibly at the City Hotel, and subsequently a chef at the Naval Academy. He purchased the freedom of his wife, her daughter, and his mother-in-law. During the 1870s, he was active in establishing Mt. Moriah A.M.E. Church on Franklin Street. The property remained in the Maynard family until Willis Burgess purchased it in 1914. It is now owned by the City of Annapolis.

*159 Duke of Gloucester Street,* built in 1917, was the home of the Independent Fire Company No. 2, the city's oldest company. The offices of the City of Annapolis Department of Planning and Zoning are located here.

*148 Duke of Gloucester Street* was built in the mid-nineteenth century as a residence and bought by William H. Butler in 1863.

Butler was a "free person of color" who owned four homes in town. He was a carpenter, builder, and landlord. He was the wealthiest African-American in Annapolis and the first to be elected to the City Council. William H. Butler, the son of the builder, continued to live in his father's house while he served on the City Council in 1892. The family lived there until 1922.

*144 Duke of Gloucester Street* was built between 1823 and 1836 as a single-family residence. After an addition in the 1930s, the building became known as the Gloucester Apartments. The original Federal/Greek Revival door trim and fanlight survives.

*128 Duke of Gloucester Street* was built in 1833, a two-story residence that would have several later additions. The lot on which number 128 stands belonged to Amos Garrett, the first mayor of Annapolis, and later passed to Dr. Charles Carroll and then to his son, Charles Carroll, the Barrister. At one time the building was used as a school.

*125 Duke of Gloucester Street* is *St. Mary's Catholic School,* a post–Civil War building in the Victorian style.

*122 Duke of Gloucester Street* was built as an office by John Ridout between 1765 and 1770. John Ridout came to Annapolis in 1753 as the secretary to the proprietary governor, Colonel Horatio Sharpe. Sharpe arrived with an entire staff: his chaplain, the Reverend Matthew Harris; his physician, Dr. Upton Scott; and Ridout. Ridout conducted the business of secretary of the province from this building when he was not in the company of the governor. Modernized with Victorian trim, it is now a residence.

*120 Duke of Gloucester Street* is the house that John Ridout built for himself and his bride, Mary Ogle, the daughter of Governor Ogle and Anne Tasker Ogle. Acccording to legend, John Ridout fell in love with Mary when she was a charming child.

John Ridout House and Carriage House, and Ridout Row,
110 to 120 Duke of Gloucester Street

Governor Sharpe was also captivated by her, but she chose the younger man. When they were married in 1764, Mary was eighteen and John was thirty-one. They had three children—Samuel, Anne, and Horatio. When Governor Sharpe returned to England, he deeded all his American properties to Ridout, including his elegant country retreat, Whitehall, just outside of Annapolis. When John Ridout died, his son Horatio inherited Whitehall and his son Samuel inherited Ridout House. One of the bedrooms is called "Colonel Sharpe's room." Ridout House is built of brick in the Georgian style. It was begun in 1764 and completed in 1765. The street facade, laid in all-header bond, is adorned by a handsome Doric entrance doorway. A second-story Palladian window interrupts the cornice on the garden side. Directly beneath this window is an elegant Doric portico. The right-hand window of the portico is a dummy and is painted black; the left-hand window is in fact a jib door. The garden, almost the same size and shape as it was in the eighteenth century, includes fine boxwood plantings. The property once ran down to the water, where Compromise Street lies today. The house is in nearly original condition, and modernization has been carried out very carefully to prevent damage to the building. George Washington and John Ridout were great friends and, until political differences made association impossible, the Washingtons and Ridouts visited together often. On her last visit, Martha Washington left her nightcap behind as a token that she hoped to return. This nightcap is still preserved in the house by John Ridout's descendants.

*116 Duke of Gloucester Street,* John Ridout's carriage house, is now a private residence. It was built in 1765 and corresponds to the office building at the other end of Ridout's street-front complex.

*110–112–114 Duke of Gloucester Street, Ridout Row,* were built in a row in 1774 by John Ridout as rental properties called tenements. They were at one time called the Three Sisters' Houses as a reminder of the days when three Ridout sisters lived side by side. They look like Georgian period town houses transplanted from a London street. The front of the center building projects beyond the others and boasts a pediment over the doorway to give the facade symmetry and the appearance of a single large Georgian mansion. In the nineteenth century this doorway was moved from its original central position to the side, and the building itself was remodeled with Greek Revival details.

The cornerstone of *St. Mary's Catholic Church* was laid on May 13, 1858, by the bishop of Philadelphia, the Most Reverend John N. Neumann, C.S.S.R.. The church was formally dedicated on January 15, 1860, but was in use as early as October 15, 1859. The architect of the Gothic Revival structure was Louis L. Long. The spire, one of the most prominent points on the Annapolis horizon, was completed in 1876. The magnificent interior was designed by members of the Redemptorist Order—the altar was carved by Brother Louis Sterkendries and the decoration painted by Brother Hilary Froehlich. This structure replaced the earlier mission church of St. Mary's, completed in 1822 and served by the Jesuits, which stood on the site of St. Mary's Hall on Duke of Gloucester Street.

*107 Duke of Gloucester Street.* To the rear of St. Mary's Church facing Spa Creek is the house of Charles Carroll, the Settler, originally built in 1680 and improved at various times until 1856. The property was purchased by Charles Carroll, the Settler, in 1701; on his death in 1720 he left a vast amount of land, much of it planted in wheat and corn rather than tobacco, to Charles Carroll of Annapolis, whose son Charles Carroll of Carrollton was the only Catholic signer of the Declaration of Independence. Charles Carroll of Carrollton was the richest man in the colonies at the time. He spent time on his estate, Doughoregan Manor in present-day Howard County, as well as in Annapolis. At his death in 1832 at ninety-five (he was the last of the signers to die), his estate was divided among his children and grandchildren. The Annapolis house, which had been rented out since 1821, was left to Carroll's daughter Mary Caton; her daughters conveyed the property to the Redemptorist Fathers for six thousand dollars in 1852. For over one hundred years of Redemptorist ownership, the Carroll House was used as a house of studies for young men preparing for the priesthood as well as a home for the local religious congregation. The rectory building itself was constructed in 1859–60. The house built by Charles Carroll of Annapolis in

1749–51 is four bays in length and delineated by the two great chimneys that still soar above the roofline. The addition to the east, built by Charles Carroll of Carrollton in 1773, was originally a passageway connecting the main block to a frame dependency that was still standing in 1858. The western addition to the house was completed in 1856. The original entrance door to the Carroll House, which faced Duke of Gloucester Street, has been incorporated into the passage leading to the present-day rectory. The interior of the house still contains some original woodwork, notably the main staircase. In the 1770s Charles Carroll of Carrollton spent a small fortune constructing a seawall of squared stones along Spa Creek and laying out terraced gardens. Much of the seawall remains, and a few traces of the terraces are still visible. After extensive restoration the house is now open to the public by appointment.

The *Annapolis Yacht Club,* built in 1963, is located at the place where Duke of Gloucester Street meets Compromise Street and Spa Creek. The Yacht Club is an outgrowth of the Severn River Boat Club, formed in 1886 as a rowing society, which rented a portion of waterfront property from St. Mary's Church. The Yacht Club actually was organized in 1918.

The point on which the Yacht Club is located may be where Robert Proctor operated a trading post about 1670. At the foot of Duke of Gloucester Street a long wooden bridge stretched across Spa Creek, linking Annapolis with the farms on Horn Point. It was replaced once in the same location with a low metal bridge with a swing arm opening. When the current drawbridge was built in 1949, the span was relocated to a terminus several blocks further west.

## CATHEDRAL STREET

Cathedral Street, which stretches from Conduit to West Street, follows the course of the seventeenth-century palisade that formed the boundary of Nicholson's Annapolis. The palisade, a fence of wooden stakes and saplings edged by a ditch, ran from Spa Creek to the City Gate at the intersection of West and Cathedral and down Calvert Street to College Creek. Palisades also protected parts of the shoreline along College Creek and near the City Dock. Originally built for protection in the case of attack, the palisade was never called on to serve this purpose. Parts of it apparently remained standing until the early nineteenth century since it is mentioned as a boundary marker in deeds of the period.

Cathedral Street was largely developed in the building boom that swept Annapolis in the 1870s, although the area around the City Gate is much older. Most of the houses were built as residences for workingmen; many of these houses are shingled.

## From Conduit Street to West Street

*1 Cathedral Street,* a long thin house built in 1869, boasts a wood-shingled mansard roof that is painted to look like slate.

*25 Cathedral Street* is an Italianate villa built by George Fiesler in 1879. Fiesler is responsible for developing most of this block: numbers 11, 17, and 19 are also attributed to him, as is 105 Conduit Street at the corner of Cathedral.

The residences of the second block of Cathedral Street are far smaller than those of the first block. Numbers *35–41 Cathedral Street* comprise a quartet of small houses sharing party walls that are unified by a single cornice. Elaborate brackets and modillions distinguish this cornice from more ordinary examples.

The third block of Cathedral Street contains the 1999 addition to the County Courthouse. Anne Arundel Medical Center was formerly located here; the hospital buildings are to be demolished. A mixed residential development is planned.

*97–99 Cathedral Street* were built between 1880 and 1890. The looped cornice and diamond-pattern mansard roof are just two of the features that render this pair of houses worthy candidates for preservation.

*106 Cathedral Street* is another post–Civil War house built in the Federal style. Now covered in aluminum siding, the house boasts the original windows, chimney, and cornice.

*113 Cathedral Street* was erected in 1820 but altered later in the nineteenth century. It is a fine example of a restored Federal town house.

*116 Cathedral Street* was constructed as a commercial building in the early nineteenth century; for many years it was used as a warehouse.

*118 Cathedral Street* was erected in the mid-nineteenth century as a commercial building with residence above, a function it still serves today. The Victorian decoration on the exterior is probably a later construction than the rest of the house.

*123–125 Cathedral Street* were built around 1760 as a double building sharing a party wall. The brick is laid in common bond with a row of headers every fifth course. The arrangement of the double porch with its built-in bench is ingenious. Both number 123 and number 125 have long histories as locations for small Annapolis businesses.

## CHARLES STREET

Charles Street is a residential side street only two blocks long that runs between Duke of Gloucester Street and Spa Creek. The buildings lining Charles Street include some of the oldest in Annapolis; most of the structures, however, date from the nineteenth and early twentieth centuries. The integrated architectural scale and the abundance of trees create a pleasant streetscape.

## From Duke of Gloucester Street to Spa Creek

*131 Charles Street,* the *Adams-Kilty House,* was built sometime between 1773 and 1786. The house is constructed in late Georgian style with brickwork laid in Flemish bond above a simple water table. A classical cornice wraps completely around the house, and two massive chimneys facing forward loom over the street. The window articulation of the Adams-Kilty House, severe in its plainness, is just one of the curious architectural details that distinguishes this house from others of the same period in Annapolis.

Because of similarities with the Chase-Lloyd House and the Hammond-Harwood House, the house has been attributed to master builder William Buckland, but there is no documentary evidence and it is unlikely since Buckland died in 1774. More likely, the house is the work of one or several craftsmen in Buckland's work force who remained in Annapolis after his death. When the Warlick family acquired the house in 1958, they returned it to single-family use and undertook a partial restoration, preserving most original finishes.

The Adams-Kilty House derives its name from two former owners. William Adams, a planter from the Eastern Shore, owned the property in 1773. William Kilty lived there in 1779 when he served as chancellor of Maryland. When Adams purchased the property it extended from the corner of Duke of Gloucester Street (then Southeast Street) to Cathedral Street, but the property was later subdivided into a number of lots.

The Adams-Kilty House was for many years the home of the Wells family. Dr. Wells is said to have attended the births of more Annapolitans than any other person.

*132 Charles Street* was begun about 1879 and an addition was built onto the north side in 1927. Both halves of the house boast fine Italianate details, for example, the cornice with its elaborate brackets and jigsaw frieze panels. This decorative grouping and the symmetrical window bays successfully distract the onlooker from noticing that the north addition is a story shorter in height than the main block. The finished bricks and fine mortar work recall numbers 32 and 36 Maryland Avenue.

*124 Charles Street* was the home of Jonas Green, founder of the *Maryland Gazette* and printer to the colony of Maryland. Green and his family published the *Gazette* on these premises for three generations.

The rear section of the house may date from as early as 1740. The gambrel-roofed structure is much like other eighteenth-century buildings in Annapolis, notably the Creagh House on Prince George Street. Jonas Green came to Annapolis in 1738 from Philadelphia, where he had been an apprentice of Benjamin Franklin. Since Annapolis at this period boasted no resident printer, Green found a ready market for his skills, and he soon entered into a long and profitable relationship with the city. In 1738 he was appointed public printer of the colony. Green belonged to the Masonic Lodge, the Jockey Club, and the Tuesday Club; he also served as a vestryman at St. Anne's Church and as a city alderman. In the words of one of his Tuesday Club associates, he was also "punchmaker-general, punster, poet, printer, and purveyor."

When he died in 1767 Green was mourned by the entire city. After her husband's death, Anne Catherine Green took over the *Gazette* and was appointed printer to the colony in her own right—the first female printer in the colonies. She was followed in the business by her sons Frederick and Samuel, who in turn were succeeded by Frederick's son Jonas. The Greens finally sold the *Gazette* about 1840.

Jonas Green House, 124 Charles Street

*120 Charles Street,* a wonderful late nineteenth-century Queen Anne structure, is typical of the houses built in wealthy eastern American suburbs at the turn of the twentieth century. Its stylized Gothic windows, diamond-shaped windowpanes, and bunched chimneys make the house unique in Annapolis.

The buildings along the remainder of the block date from the post–Civil War boom period, and the scale of all the structures is complementary. All are Victorian in style, though two or three sport Federal or Greek Revival details. The shingled houses form one of the nicest features of Annapolis. The lower block of Charles Street is lined by the same type of buildings but on a smaller scale; many of these houses are attached. At 95 Charles Street, a fine example shows how the Victorians assimilated Greek Revival features into their own aesthetic.

## *CONDUIT STREET*

Conduit Street derives its name from the fact that in the eighteenth century it provided a passage, or conduit, from Main Street to Duke of Gloucester Street. It originally ran only one block; in the 1870s, however, the street was extended to Spa Creek in order to provide access to the new lots behind Market Street that were developed in the post–Civil War building boom. The new section of Conduit Street swings slightly to the southwest. The building at *179 Duke of Gloucester* lost two of its five bays when the street was put through.

### From Main Street to Spa Creek

*The Pinkney-Callahan House, 164 Conduit Street,* originally stood on the corner of Bladen Street (formerly called Lawyer's Street) and College Avenue (formerly Tabernacle Street). The house was built about 1785 by the Callahan family on a lot purchased by John Callahan at the time of his marriage to Sarah Buckland. Sarah was the daughter of William Buckland, who designed the Hammond-Harwood House. It was a substantial building of brick, as befitted its builder, who is mentioned in Christopher Richmond's account of services rendered to Maryland troops during the Revolution. The garden extended from College Avenue to State Circle. John Callahan served as "Commissioner of the Land Office of the Western Shore of Maryland." He died in 1803, and Sarah continued to live in the house until 1839 when she sold it to Somerville Pinkney.

In the early 1900s, the State of Maryland decided to erect a new Court of Appeals building on the site of the old Callahan house. The occupants of the house, the Pinkney sisters, arranged to relocate the structure to the St. John's College campus three hundred feet away. They continued to live in the house while it was being moved, a process that took six weeks, and they served tea each afternoon to friends and passersby. St. John's College bought the house in 1928 and used it as an infirmary for many years.

In 1972 St. John's planned to convert the site of the house to another use and the structure was moved to 164 Conduit Street. It now screens the Gorman Street parking garage from view and is used for offices.

The floor plan of the Pinkney-Callahan House is similar to that of Ogle Hall. It has fine brickwork, an elegant stairway, and a doorway probably based on a plate from eighteenth-century designer Batty Langley's *City and Country Builders and Workmen's Treasury of Designs,* printed in London in 1750.

*162 Conduit Street* was built as a fine hostelry by George N. Mann in 1787. It was an addition to his succcessful City Hotel, which faced Main Street. The hotel was originally the Dulaney-Woodward house. Mann bought that building after the Revolution as it had been confiscated from Loyalist Lloyd Dulaney by the State of Maryland. The Conduit Street hotel building is a prominent three-story, five-bay building of brick laid in Flemish bond. Although clearly Georgian in form and material, the interior woodwork is distinctly Federal. George Mann operated the tavern in the hotel until his death in 1795. He had leased the hotel business to James Wharfe just before his death. His wife Mary Buckland, daughter of William Buckland, who designed the Hammond-Harwood House, lived in the Conduit Street building and paid taxes on it in 1798. She died in 1810 and a long chancery court case delayed the transfer of the house to the Manns' two daughters. After two years, they advertised the building for sale. The property passed through many hands in the nineteenth century until it was finally purchased by Lodge 89 of the Associated Free Masons, who have used if for their meetings and ceremonies for over one hundred years.

The City Hotel annex *(150–160 Conduit Street),* a six-section rowhouse block attached to Mann's Tavern, was probably initiated when John Walton acquired the property in 1848. Walton's tenure was one of the longest in the nineteenth century, extending to 1871 when he died.

George Washington stayed at Mann's hotel in December 1783 when he came to Annapolis to resign his commission as commander in chief of the Continental Army. The hotel remained a fashionable place throughout the nineteenth century under the name City Hotel. It closed in 1900 and burned down shortly thereafter.

*163–165 Conduit Street.* In the late eighteenth century Moses MacCubbin sold "cosmetics, soap, tooth paste, Powder Horns, combs, waters, pomades" at his shop on this site. The building now on the site is a Federal style dating from 1810–15 and is a good example of the type of commercial structure erected all over Annapolis during the early nineteenth century.

The corner of Conduit and Duke of Gloucester Streets, now occupied by the *First Presbyterian Church,* was the site of the City Theater from 1828 to 1847. This theater replaced the eighteenth-century structure on West Street that was demolished in 1818; the cornerstone from the old theater was incorporated into the new building. A leaden box containing, among other things, a copy of George Washington's will, was placed under the cornerstone. The City Theater was demolished in 1847 to build the original First Presbyterian Church. When this structure was enlarged and rebuilt in 1946, the south wall of the nave from the 1848 church was retained and can be viewed from the narrow alleyway. The roof over the nave also remains and is signed by the carpenter Daniel Sprogle.

*138 Conduit Street,* an example of the Queen Anne/Eastlake style, was constructed as a residence in 1887 by Professor Charles A. Zimmerman, bandmaster at the Naval Academy. Zimmerman, who held the post of bandmaster for over twenty years, composed "Anchors Aweigh" during his residence at number 138. Prominent architectural features include a pyramidal turret which crowns a two-story bay window, a conical turret which tops a half-story tower, the decorative cove, patterned wood shingles, and a patterned masonry chimney. The house was designed by architect George Barer of Knoxville, Tennessee and published in his 1891 book of plans, *The Cottage Souvenir No. 2.*

*105 Conduit Street* may have been built around 1866 by George Fiesler. The house is constructed in the Federal style, even though the style was out-of-date by then. This phenomenon was typical in Annapolis, since the city tended to lag behind current architectural trends.

The remaining buildings on the middle block of Conduit Street were all built in the 1870s and 1880s. Many of them were erected in pairs by a builder who would live in one and rent or sell the other. For this reason, one of the pair often boasts more elaborate exterior decoration than the other. All these houses are Victorian or Federal in detail. The graceful streetscape of this block derives from the unified scale of its residences.

The block of Conduit Street stretching from Cathedral Street down the hill to Spa Creek also dates from the late nineteenth century. Because of the steepness of the slope many of the houses on the west side of the street seem to perch rather precariously above garages and basement stories. The streetscape is in some ways more reminiscent of a New England port town than one found in a mid-Atlantic location. Two houses deserve special attention. Number 98 sports some fascinating details, including a cornice with brackets, dentils, and various jigsaw patterns. The 1920s porch with Tuscan columns is a typical alteration. Number 82 Conduit Street is covered with late Victorian fish-scale shingles. The four Tuscan columns of the porch support the projecting temple pediment.

## MARKET STREET

Market Street is one of the streets laid out in the survey of Annapolis by James Stoddert in 1718. It runs from Duke of Gloucester Street down a considerable hill to Spa Creek. The original 1696 plan for the town called for wharfage to be built on the waterfront so that produce could be brought up the hill to stock the city market, which was to be erected at the intersection of Market and Duke of Gloucester Streets. A market was to be held each week and a fair each year. Though that plan was never executed, the street name remains as a reminder.

### From Duke of Gloucester Street to Spa Creek

By 1720 at least two houses were on the street. *Number 139 Market Street* may have been built as early as the first half of the eighteenth century. Records show that it was owned in 1720 by Thomas Larkin and in 1762 by John Hall. The house has long been called "Charles Carroll the Settler House," but recent research has proven this name to be in error, since Charles Carroll lived on Duke of Gloucester Street in 1718. The building was built in three phases. The oldest portion is the three-bay southeastern section of the current structure. Although now clad with brick, this was originally a one-story frame building.

*110–112 Market Street* were built about 1840 in the Greek Revival style as residences.

*100 Market Street* is a small, brown-shingled house that may have been built in the early eighteenth century. The interior has been adapted to modern living in a contemporary style.

Most of the other residences along Market Street date from the period after 1870 when lots were sold off wholesale. In the period of a year, three hundred houses were built from Spa Creek on the southeast to South Street on the southwest. Most are late nineteenth-century Victorian buildings, built of frame with various kinds of details—Italianate, Federal, and Greek Revival.

## SHIPWRIGHT STREET

### From Market Street to Spa Creek

*Upton Scott House, 4 Shipwright Street.* A native of Ireland, Dr. Upton Scott came to Annapolis in 1753 as physician to Governor Horatio Sharpe. Also in the party was John Ridout, the governor's young secretary. They arrived on the ship *Molly* on August 10. Dr. Scott, about thirty years old at the time, soon married Elizabeth Ross of Frederick County, Maryland. Construction on the house began about 1762, although Scott had purchased the land in 1759. His undertaker was William Brown, a joiner and carpenter who had just built his house and tavern on the South River at London Town.

The Upton Scott House, as it is called today, is a large Georgian structure that retains most of its original material. The brick walls on a stone foundation are laid in header bond on the front and garden elevations and Flemish bond on the sides, although the dormers on the southwestern elevation are later additions. As is typical of important eighteenth-century gentry town houses in Annapolis, the garden elevation is as important as the elevation facing the street or in this case the land dropping down to Spa Creek. Dr. Scott's hobby was botany and he had large gardens extending to Duke of Gloucester Street. He also maintained green-

Upton Scott House, 4 Shipwright Street

houses filled with rare plants and shrubs. The rooms on the garden side are the more finely finished and clearly intended for entertaining. On either side of the Shipwright Street elevation of the house are two surviving outbuildings, remnants of plantation-inspired architecture in the city. The building on the west side was used as a stable and the altered two-story residential building on the east side was probably the carriage house. A wash house survived until the mid-1990s.

During the Revolution, Dr. Scott was probably a Loyalist. He left Annapolis in 1776, only to return in 1780. In 1783 his friend, Governor Robert Eden, returned to Annapolis to try to obtain restitution of his property, which had been confiscated by the State of Maryland in 1776. He stayed at Dr. Scott's house for only a short time; he never recovered his land and died soon after his arrival. Both gentlemen were much admired by the citizens of the town despite their political beliefs. Elihu Riley said that Dr. Scott died on February 23, 1814, and described him as having a career "of unbroken virtue, dignity and usefulness." Dr. Scott is buried in St. Anne's Cemetery, while Governor Eden is buried in St. Anne's churchyard.

Dr. Scott and his wife had no children, but their great-nephew, Francis Scott Key, lived at the house for seven years while he attended St. John's College. In 1814 he wrote the national anthem after watching the bombardment of Fort McHenry in Baltimore.

Winston Churchill (a very distant American cousin of the British prime minister) probably had Dr. Scott's house in mind when he wrote his novel *Richard Carvel*. Richard, the hero, lived at the Upton Scott house, and the William Paca house was the home of Dorothy Manners, the heroine. Churchill grew interested in colonial Annapolis during his four years as a midshipman at the Naval Academy. *Richard Carvel,* published in 1899, was a best-seller. Churchill's subsequent novels were less popular and these are all but forgotten today.

For many years the Upton Scott House was owned by St. Mary's Church and used as a convent by the Sisters of Notre Dame. It is now a private residence.

## *GREEN STREET*

### From Duke of Gloucester Street to the Dock

Green Street was opened for development by Dr. Charles Carroll in 1752. It runs one block from Church Street (now Main

Street) to Duke of Gloucester Street. Lots were for sale on both sides of the street.

*Number 183,* the oldest house on Green Street, is near the intersection with Main Street. The frame building on this site was probably built in the late eighteenth century, but its builder remains a mystery. In 1784 the house was leased to Adam Reb, who turned over his lease to Simon Retallick. In 1788 records show that Retallick was living in a house on Green Street, probably number 183. The house is called "the Ironmaster's House." Simon Retallick was of French descent and worked as a blacksmith. He did ironwork for the State House, the Chase-Lloyd House, and the Treasury Building as well as common household items for townspeople and shipowners. He married a Brewer, related to John Brewer of Cornhill Street. The house descended in the Brewer family for at least five generations.

In 1805 the Farmers National Bank opened its offices at *160 Green Street*. Articles of association to establish the bank were printed the year before, but the act of assembly was passed in 1805. Books were opened on July 16, and in two days 1,690 shares were sold in the Annapolis Assembly Rooms on Duke of Gloucester Street. The building is now a residence and the bank's main branch is on Church Circle.

Though Dr. Charles Carroll hoped to develop his lots in 1752, most of the remaining buildings date from the late nineteenth century. They are residences, many with typical Annapolis brown-shingled siding often covering original German siding and trim of various Victorian styles. The building at *172 Green Street* was built about 1840 and resembles a Charleston single house with side piazza.

The *Annapolis Elementary School* at *180 Green Street* began in a dwelling bought from the Stockett family about 1880. That building was originally the town house of Dr. Charles Carroll and his son, Charles Carroll, the Barrister. The stone wall at street level probably dates from their time. The property provided space for an elementary school, a high school, and, from time to time, the offices for the board of education. Public education in Annapolis began on the site of the school, which has undergone many renovations as the years have passed. The first graduating class at the high school was that of 1899.

In the nineteenth century Green Street was notorious as the haunt of a headless man who wandered every night from Duke of Gloucester Street to the Market Place and back. Perhaps he was seeking the spectral horse loaded with chains that galloped down Main Street every night during the same period. The best-known sighting of the headless man occurred during the Spanish-American War when a prominent soft-shell crabber named Lowman ran smack into him while en route to his boat. Lowman, scared out of his wits, was left prostrate; the ghost perhaps was equally terrified as he has not appeared in Annapolis since.

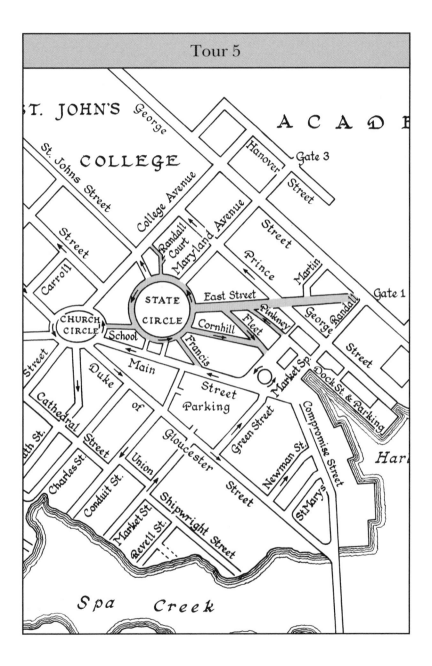

# State Circle, Randall Court, and School, Francis, Cornhill, Fleet, East, and Pinkney Streets

## *STATE CIRCLE*

When the Annapolis town plan was first drawn in 1696, State Circle was conceived as the center of all state government buildings. The State House was to be in the center of the circle, the armory on its right, and King William's School on its left and to the rear. Also in the rear of the circle was the "public temple," otherwise known as the public privy. The original privy was replaced sometime between 1780 and 1790 by an octagonal one designed by Joseph Clark and furnished by John Shaw. Jubb Fowler was paid seven shillings and six pence to clean out "the temple" in 1792. By 1854 it had fallen into such disrepair that it was called a "disgustingly conspicuous building" and was ordered demolished. That did not happen, however, until 1905.

Today State House Hill is capped by the capitol building and, flanking it to the right, the treasury building. The Maryland Legislature meets in the State House from January to April each year, making the Maryland State House the oldest state capitol building in continuous use by its legislature.

## State House and Old Treasury Building

The first *State House* in Annapolis was completed in 1698. Called the "Stadt House" in honor of the Dutch-born King William, the building was struck by lightning in 1699, killing one of the delegates. Many early records were destroyed in the resulting fire. In

1704 the State House was again engulfed by fire, and all the records were lost.

In 1705 the second State House was begun on the foundations of the old building, and the new one was in use by 1707. By 1766, however, this building had fallen into a state of disrepair; since it was also very small and architecturally undistinguished, it was deemed most reasonable to tear down the entire structure and begin anew. By 1772 plans for the third State House had been drawn by Joseph Horatio Anderson, and construction was undertaken by Charles Wallace. The cornerstone was laid by Governor Eden, the last proprietary governor of Maryland, on March 28, 1772. Wallace engaged William Buckland to assist him, perhaps to design or carve the woodwork of the Old Senate Chamber. Construction progressed smoothly and the building was already in use when a hurricane in September 1774 destroyed the copper roof and damaged the cupola. The next year Charles Wallace began construction of a new roof with a steeper pitch, and this time it was covered with wooden shingles.

By the advent of the Revolution, Charles Wallace had spent three years working on the State House. He found workmen and materials equally difficult to procure and, in frustration, he resigned. At that time the building was nearly complete inside and out, but the cupola had still not been shingled, and rain damaged it badly. Nonetheless, the Maryland General Assembly met in the State House in 1779, and it was used by both county and city governments for offices.

The year 1783 was a memorable one for Annapolis. The Continental Congress met there for nine months, from November 26, 1783, to August 13, 1784; thus Annapolis served the new nation as its capital. Patriotic emotion peaked on December 23, 1783, when General George Washington appeared before the Continental Congress to resign his commission as commander in chief of the Continental Army. The evening before the formal

Maryland State House, State Circle

resignation, Governor William Paca hosted a fete at which the citizens of Annapolis greeted and congratulated the beloved hero. George Mann, proprietor of Mann's Hotel, "furnished the supper at the State House," which included "ninety-eight bottles of wine, two and one-half gallons of spirits, nine pounds of sugar, a lot of limes, music and waiters, and a dozen packs of cards." The State of Maryland provided entertainment for the populace. They bought "from James Makubbin a hogshead of rum (116 gallons at 6s. 6d. per gallon)" and from George Mann, "49 gallons of claret, 32 gallons of Madeira, 35 of port, 6 of spirit." Food must also have been plentiful for this spectacular event. There were "15 lb. of loaf sugar, 176 lb. of bacon, 284 lb. of salt beef, 52 lb. of shoat, 126 lb. of mutton, 272 lb. of veal, 183 lb. of beef, 7 lambs, and 12 fowls." For the ball that closed the day there were "8 gallons of wine, 4 of spirits, beef, hams, tongues, chickens, turkeys, tarts, custards, cheese-cakes, 502 loaves of bread, 24 shillings worth of cards, and a box of candles." The state had to "pay Mr. Mann for 35 knives and 29 forks lost, and 28 plates, 49 wine glasses, 1 dish, 61 broken bottles."

Peace came formally on January 14, 1784, with the ratification of the Treaty of Paris by the Continental Congress. This occasion was greeted with very little fanfare. In May of 1784 Thomas Jefferson was appointed minister plenipotentiary to France, meaning that he was a United States diplomat with full powers to deal with foreign governments.

All of this activity took place in the still unfinished State House. In 1785 Joseph Clark undertook to finish the work on the roof and to rebuild the cupola. Much interior finishing needed to be done, as well as decorating and furnishing.

In 1786 the Annapolis Convention, a prologue to the Constitutional Convention of the following year, was held from September 11 to 14 at Mann's Hotel. No Maryland delegates attended. That year the Maryland General Assembly agreed to pay passage for Irish carpenters to finish the dome and staircase. The staircase leads to the dome, where a lantern was hung when the legislature was in session. This custom of lighting the dome is still followed today.

In 1787 the state again ran out of funds to work on the building, and little more was accomplished until 1792 when contracts were let to William Gilmour for carpentry work and to Thomas Dance for plastering. Dance fell from the dome and was killed in 1793. At that time, the cabinetmaker John Shaw took over the work which was finally nearing completion. In 1796 the commission for the Senate Chamber furniture was given to John Shaw.

By 1858 the requirements of state government had increased to such a degree that an annex to the Court of Appeals room was constructed in an octagonal shape. Fifteen years later the building had fallen into such a dreadful state of repair that funds were appropriated to make extensive renovations. The floors of the Old Senate Chamber were rotted, and the ceiling above sagged. The Old Senate Chamber was stripped of its beautiful old cornice and carvings and was refurnished in the modern style of the day. The "hue and cry" which followed this disaster eventually made it necessary for Governor Edwin Warfield to appoint J. Appleton Wilson of Baltimore and Frank Mayer of Annapolis to investigate and plan the restoration of the Old Senate Chamber. The work was begun in 1902. At that time the northwest addition was made to the State House to provide new, more spacious chambers for the Senate and the House of Delegates. In 1948 the state received the eighteenth-century president's chair and desk and in 1964 one of the member's desks as gifts. The other desks and chairs in the Old Senate Chamber are fine reproductions of the work of John Shaw, whose shop was just across State Circle from the room for which the pieces were made.

As early as 1781 the legislature of Maryland was interested in decorating the State House with paintings and other art important to state history. In that year the legislature requested Charles Willson Peale to paint a full-length portrait of General George Washington "in grateful Remembrance of that most illustrious character." Peale painted Washington with Tench Tilghman, Washington's aide-de-camp, representing the State of Maryland, and General Lafayette representing the alliance with France. The painting still hangs over the fireplace of the Old Senate Chamber, where it was placed when Peale finished it. The State House also boasts other Peale portraits of early governors, modern portraits of Maryland signers of the Declaration of Independence, two paintings commissioned of Frank Mayer depicting incidents from the state's early history, and other works in various areas of the building. The silver service made by Samuel Kirk and Company of Baltimore in 1906 for use on the armored cruiser USS *Maryland* is also on display in the State House. The service was transferred to the battleship *Maryland* in 1921 and, since that ship's decommissioning, it has been carefully preserved, first by the Maryland Historical Society and now by the State of Maryland.

The *Old Treasury Building* was built between 1735 and 1737 by Patrick Creagh. The building was to serve as an office for the Commissioners for Emitting Bills of Credit, or paper money. The commission met on Wednesdays to distribute ninety thousand pounds, Maryland money, in bills to relieve the problems caused by the tobacco currency then in use. Since tobacco was bulky and difficult to change, Maryland suffered from a severe shortage of circulating money in the eighteenth century.

From 1779 to 1851 the building served as the offices of the Treasurer of the Western Shore. When the treasuries from both the eastern and western shores were merged in 1852, the new state treasurer occupied the offices. During the latter half of the nineteenth century the Old Treasury Building served as a storeroom for old papers and memorabilia. In 1884 state officials hunting for relics to commemorate the 250th anniversary of the founding of Maryland discovered the 1648 seal of the colony, long presumed lost, in a corner of the Old Treasury Building. In 1903 the treasurer vacated the building. It was turned over to the department of education and subsequently was occupied by a number of state agencies in succession.

The brick building is cruciform, or cross-shaped, in form. It probably looks much like the old state capital built at St. Mary's City in the 1630s. The brick is laid in Flemish bond, the roof is steep, and the windows are small and barred. The building was restored in 1949 and looks much as it did when it was first completed.

## Around State Circle from School Street

*Government House,* the residence of Maryland's governors, was built in 1868 and was remodeled into a five-part Georgian Revival mansion in 1936. Government House is furnished with Maryland art and furniture, with a different period represented in each of the public rooms. The Maryland Historical Society assists with this ongoing project.

The original 1868 residence was in the Second Empire Revival style, made of brick with a French mansard roof. Tall windows lighted the two main floors. The rooftop belvedere and extensive porches made enjoyment of the large garden possible. When the building was "Georgianized" in the 1930s, the porches were removed and symmetrical hyphens and wings added in their place. The visitor can still detect at least one surviving Victorian feature, a two-story bay window, on the College Avenue elevation of the house.

Before the erection of Government House, this site was occupied by two imposing eighteenth-century mansions. One of these houses was the home of the Ridgely family. Absalom Ridgely, a merchant, began his business career in the small building at the corner of Fleet and Cornhill Streets; by the time of his death in 1818 he had become one of the wealthiest citizens of Annapolis. The house passed to his son John, who had served as surgeon on the USS *Philadelphia* when it was captured by the Pasha of Tripoli in 1804. Ridgely and his shipmates were

rescued by Stephen Decatur the following year, but not before
the doctor had saved the children of the pasha from a serious
illness. In gratitude, the pasha gave Ridgely a fine Arabian
horse; the doctor brought the steed back with him and thereafter delighted in riding it through the streets of Annapolis.

Beginning in the 1930s, the state purchased much of the
land west of the State House and erected a number of pseudo-
colonial buildings for government offices. The design and work-
manship of these buildings are of generally high quality, but
they are much larger than anything erected in Annapolis in the
colonial period. To show this difference in scale, the massive
Lowe Office Building on Rowe Boulevard can be compared with
the intimate size of the Old Treasury Building.

*23 State Circle,* known today as the *Robert Johnson House,* was built
as a residence by John Johnson, Jr., in 1773. Johnson was chancellor of the state and was the grandfather-in-law of John Quincy
Adams.

*21 State Circle,* the *Brooksby-Shaw House,* dates from about 1720.
Cornelius Brooksby purchased the lot from goldsmith John
Steele for 25 pounds sterling in 1720 and began construction on
his large, gambrel-roofed house, but it was not completed until
two years after his death. His "relict," as widows were called
then, married Thomas Gough, and they were living in the house
in 1725. In 1740 the house was owned by Sewell Long, a sailor
and shipwright who had married Mary Brooksby, the granddaughter of the builder. In 1784 David Long, Sewell's son, sold
the house to John Shaw for 510 pounds sterling. Shaw operated
his cabinetmaking business from this building. He had previously had a partner, but when the partnership was dissolved in
1776, he set up business on Pinkney Street, near the Slicer
House. Fire destroyed that shop in 1782. He made repairs for
Thomas Jefferson in the State Circle building, since Jefferson
notes that he paid Shaw for some repairs when he was here dur-

ing the meeting of the Continental Congress. Shaw may also have ordered the "green Baise" cloth for the table in the Old Senate Chamber on which the Treaty of Paris was ratified in 1784. When Shaw died the property was left to his five children and remained in their hands until 1901. (The widow's walk was added to the house between 1820 and 1835.) Francis Scott Key visited the younger Dr. Shaw there. The house was possibly the site of the wedding of Anne Franklin and Lieutenant Winfield Schley, who later became Admiral Schley of Spanish-American War fame. After passing out of the Shaw family, the house served as an Elks lodge until it was bought by the State of Maryland. The second-story woodwork and the doorframes on the entry level are of the original pegged construction. The spiral staircase to the basement and the stairway leading to the upper floor are also original. The cooking fireplace is in the basement. The impressive front porch, which runs the length of the facade, was added by the Elks.

*17 State Circle,* the *Franklin Law Office,* was built of wood about 1850 to serve as a law office for James Shaw Franklin, a descendant of John Shaw. James returned from the Civil War to practice law there until his death in 1881. The temple front and elegant neoclassical fittings exemplify the Greek Revival style of architecture. It is one of the few examples in Annapolis. The building has served many purposes over the years but still remains a small, two-room office.

*1 State Circle* is an early nineteenth-century building of clapboard with a large central chimney. Constructed by property owner James Williams, the building was intended to be leased as commercial space, a use it has continued to maintain for nearly two hundred years.

*50 State Circle* is a late eighteenth-century building intended for commercial purposes. Its brick is laid in Flemish bond. The mansard roof is a post–Civil War modification; photographs taken about 1860 show a peaked roof hidden by a stepped pediment that is Flemish in inspiration. The windows in the newer attic story do not correspond to those in the five bays on the two lower floors.

*58 State Circle* is the *Governor Calvert House*. Built in the 1720s, it has been altered over the years. In the nineteenth century it was a residence for the Claude family, and eventually it became an apartment for Claude descendants. Charles Calvert, governor of Maryland from 1720 to 1727, owned the land during his residence in Annapolis. He is said to have built a small frame dwelling on the property, but its exact location is unknown. In 1982 the University of Maryland began archaeological excavations in the cellar and around the foundations of the house. The team uncovered a hypocaust (a heating tunnel) that may date from the ownership of Charles Calvert or of his brother Benedict Leonard, governor from 1727 to 1731.

*64 State Circle* was the office of Dr. Dennis Claude, who died in December 1863 "at an advanced age." He was followed in service to the community by Dr. Abram Claude, who was mayor of the city in 1883.

*86–88 State Circle,* a duplex, was built by Alexander Randall in 1878 in the English Queen Anne style. The paneled chimney, terra-cotta wall shingles, and vertical emphasis typify the style.

*90 State Circle,* the *Legislative Services Building,* was erected in 1976 in the Georgian Revival style favored by the state for its modern offices. The small scale of this building is well attuned to its setting on State Circle, and the simple design is closer to the style of eighteenth-century Annapolis than that of other new state buildings. From 1903 to 1972 this site was occupied by the Court of Appeals Building, a Beaux Arts structure. The Court of Appeals boasted a classical portico and a flight of steps echoing those of the State House across the street. The interior was paneled in mahogany. The paneling and ornamental plasterwork from the ceiling of the old courtroom were preserved and installed in the new court structure, the Court of Appeals Building on Rowe Boulevard.

Just off the back porch of the State House and next to the Governor's Mansion is the Thurgood Marshall Memorial, which is actually on Lawyers Mall. It was dedicated in 1996 and honors Thurgood Marshall, the first black Supreme Court justice. As an attorney his most famous case was *Brown v. Board of Education of Topeka (1954)*. He served the court for twenty-four years.

## RANDALL COURT

### Between State Circle and College Avenue

*Bordley-Randall House, 9 Randall Court,* sits in the center of the parklike Randall Court; access is through a Victorian gateway. Thomas Bordley built a house on this site and it was inventoried upon his death in 1727. However, the inventory does not correspond with the present house, and it is likely that his son and heir, Stephen, built the first part of the present house about 1760 while he was the attorney general.

Charles Willson Peale painted Thomas Bordley's daughter Elizabeth in 1770. The house, with its tall columns, was in the background. When Stephen Bordley and his sister Elizabeth lived in the house, the tract included the entire block from Northeast Street (Maryland Avenue) to North Street, about four acres. There were extensive gardens and all the outbuildings necessary to make the estate nearly self-sufficient.

Stephen Bordley was educated in England for the bar. He was a lifelong bachelor—sophisticated and urbane—and a connoisseur of books, wine, and fine furnishings. He died in

1764, and the house passed to Stephen's younger half-brother, John Beale Bordley, also a lawyer. The house was occupied by Elizabeth during Beale Bordley's ownership, since he preferred his estates on the Eastern Shore and his wife's home in Philadelphia to Annapolis. His wife was a member of the prominent Chew family of Philadelphia.

When Elizabeth Bordley died in 1789, Beale Bordley rented the house to John Johnson, chancellor of Maryland, whose son, Reverdy Johnson, was born there in 1796. Reverdy Johnson, one of the most prominent Marylanders of his day, served in the United States Senate from 1845 to 1849 and again from 1863 to 1868. In 1849 he was appointed attorney general of the United States by Zachary Taylor; in 1856 he was one of the lawyers who argued the Dred Scott case before the Supreme Court. Johnson's public career culminated in his appointment in 1868 as United States minister to England. In this capacity he negotiated an agreement to recompense northern merchants for damages inflicted by Confederate privateers, such as James Waddell's *Shenandoah,* outfitted in British ports during the Civil War. Johnson returned to Annapolis in 1869. He died in February 1876 of injuries sustained when he fell off the front porch of Government House after leaving a state dinner.

In 1798 Philip Barton Key rented the College Avenue wing as an office, and his nephew, Francis Scott Key, read for the bar with him there. Beale Bordley died in 1804, and the property was bought by John Johnson, who began to subdivide the large lot in 1811. By 1845 the divisions had become so complex that a lawsuit resulted; the house was ultimately sold to Alexander Randall, the son of John Randall (see 86–88 State Circle). Alexander Randall began making changes to the house, adding a portion to the rear and a room over the porch. Alexander was the father of fourteen children, and so the need to enlarge an already large house is understandable. The house was called the Homestead when the Randalls lived there.

In 1939 the house was purchased by Captain Phillip V. H. Weems, the developer of a celestial navigation system. Weems prepared Charles Lindberg for his flight to Paris in 1927, and he came out of retirement to teach the same system to John Glenn for his travel into space. The house remained in the Weems family until 2002.

## SCHOOL STREET

### From Church Circle to State Circle

School Street takes its name from King William's School, which was located on State Circle across the street. The buildings which originally stood along School Street have disappeared and have been replaced by commercial structures used as professional offices, apartments , and an inn. The street, only one block long, connects Church Circle to State Circle.

## FRANCIS STREET

Francis Street is named for Governor Francis Nicholson, who is responsible for the 1696 plan of Annapolis. The street runs one short block to connect Main Street with State Circle. When William Paca was governor in 1782, he traveled by barge from his wharf on King George Street to the foot of Francis Street. He then walked in a stately manner to his office at the State House. The streets were dirty and foul smelling, but this ritual gave the populace a chance to see and greet their governor.

### From Main Street to State Circle

*10 Francis Street,* known as the Indian King Tavern in 1774, incorporates at least four periods of construction ranging from the first quarter of the eighteenth century through the mid-nineteenth century. The building began in the early eighteenth century as a single-room plan (the front west or left side) with masonry walls. This gable-roofed structure was probably built by Henry Donaldson, who began paying rent on the property to King William's School (now St. John's College) in 1730. The house was subsequently leased to Dr. George Stuart from 1738 to 1773, who, during his tenure, enlarged it to create a center-passage one-room-deep dwelling. Dr. Stuart subleased the house to innkeeper Isaac McHard. It was during this period that the building was doubled in depth to form a Georgian plan for use as a tavern and inn as the "Sign of the Indian King." McHard, an active member of a local committee involved in planning the American Revolution, provided a venue for their meetings. The Indian King Tavern remained an inn until 1821. It was not until 1854 that St. John's College transferred ownership of the property into private hands and John Walton was able to purchase it. The Walton family brought the house up to date during the mid-nineteenth century. Their changes included the bay window and the Italianate detailing at the cornice, the rusticated foundation, and the scored plaster finish. Walton descendants owned the property until 1948.

*8 Francis Street* was built in 1878 by Tribe No. 38, Improved Order of Redmen, a patriotic organization that traces its roots back to the Sons of Liberty. Founded in Maryland, it is the oldest organization of its kind in the United States. The fraternal organization constructed this combination commercial building and social hall in the Italianate style with a handsome Venetian window to illuminate the two-story meeting space. Although not original, the present window replaces an unsightly alteration that filled half the openings with brick topped with metal windows.

## CORNHILL STREET

The land through which Cornhill and Fleet Streets run today was originally surveyed for the use of Governor Nicholson, who intended to use it for a garden, vineyard, and summerhouse. Nicholson apparently did build a small frame structure on the property, but its location has not been determined. In 1770, the property was sold to Charles Wallace by the Bordley family, who had acquired it in a slightly unsavory fashion after Nicholson's departure from Annapolis. After the destruction of all the Annapolis land records in the State House fire of 1704, two enterprising men—Thomas Bordley and Thomas Larkin—decided to claim the entire city as their own. The original property owners found themselves forced to pay Bordley and Larkin to secure their titles. Although the courts finally rejected the Bordley-Larkin claim in 1733, the pair had in the interim amassed a tidy profit by their quick thinking.

Charles Wallace laid out lots along streets named Fleet and Cornhill after two busy mercantile streets in London. Wallace hoped to build warehouses and stores along the water's edge, with a new wharf where shallow-draft barges would transfer goods from ships out in the Severn. The area along the wharf was marshy and unnavigable by oceangoing vessels.

Cornhill Street runs from State Circle to the waterfront. Its name was taken from Cornhill in London, the street on which the grain exchange was located. The Annapolis namesake was an artisan's street with a workingman's tavern and the homes of a silversmith and a coach maker. At an earlier time there was even a "ropewalk," where hemp was twisted into rope for the shipping industry. The buildings date from the late seventeenth to the late nineteenth century.

## From Market Space to State Circle

*6–8 Cornhill Street* was originally Caton's Barber Shop. It was constructed around 1790 as two individual buildings on land that was developed by Charles Wallace, a former staymaker and merchant. The buildings were merged in the early twentieth century and modernized with a mansard roof. The area then

Residences on Cornhill Street, between State Circle and Market Space

became known as Flatiron Corner, a reference to the merged building's resemblance to the more famous New York office building.

In 1919, Roger Williams, an African-American entrepreneur, purchased the property and operated a barbershop. He refused to sell his property during the 1970s when urban renewal displaced many black families in the neighborhood. After his death in 1983, Roger Williams's barbershop was touted as the last black establishment in the area.

*10–12 Cornhill Street* was built between 1774 and 1798 by Absalom Ridgely, a local storekeeper and land holder in Annapolis. Later the property was occupied by John Chalmers, a silversmith and engraver.

*14–26 and 32–34 Cornhill Street* are typical Annapolis row houses, built in the mid- to late nineteenth century for workingmen.

*30 Cornhill Street* is the focal point at the top of Hyde's Alley, which runs from Cornhill to Main Street. Built about 1798, the house was occupied by the carriage maker Samuel Hutton and features panel shutters and beaded board siding, typical eighteenth-century details.

*38–40 Cornhill Street* are two residences owned by one family. Number 40, dating from about 1775, is a Georgian-style structure that was operated as a boardinghouse. In 1900, William J. Contee, an African-American sailor in the U.S. Navy, purchased the property.

*37–39 Cornhill Street* was one building in 1772 when it was built by John Brewer for use as a residence and a tavern. During the Annapolis session of the Continental Congress in 1783–84, Thomas Jefferson made references in his diary to arrangements made to accommodate his groom and horses with John Brewer. The house was divided in the nineteenth century and is now two residences.

*41 Cornhill Street* was built between 1771 and 1773 by Captain Beriah Maybury. The Italianate dwelling was used as the Kings' Arms Tavern.

*49 Cornhill Street* was built in 1770 of clapboard, much like number 53 but obviously smaller. It has a gambrel roof and unfortunately has been reduced by about a third of its original size to make room for a driveway. It was built by carpenter William Munroe.

*53 Cornhill Street,* the *Callahan House,* was built about 1770. It has a gambrel roof and massive end chimneys. It was probably built by William Munroe, who lived in the small home at number 49 Cornhill Street.

*54–56–58 Cornhill Street* are three Federal town houses built in 1821 by Jeremiah Hughes, who rented or "let" them out. The buildings continued to be used as rental property by nine-teenth- and twentieth-century owners.

*57 Cornhill Street,* the *McCusker House,* possibly was built in the late eighteenth century and shows the architectural details of various periods of construction, including Federal and Victorian styles. The wonderful "semi-detached" chimneys are out-standing features of this house. Called the McCusker House after the family who owned it for over one hundred years, it was sold by them in 1995.

*60 Cornhill Street* is part of a row of rental houses, but it was occupied by the owner, Jeremiah Hughes. In the Victorian period the roof of the house was raised to accommodate a large family. The basic structure is Federal in design, and the addition is Victorian. The original doorway has been converted into a window; the present entrance is a modern but harmonious modification. A delightful garden and a balcony are snuggled behind the cliff-like back wall of the Circle Theater.

## FLEET STREET

Fleet Street is a little alleyway that runs from East Street to Cornhill and then flows into the Market Space. It has also been called Taylor Street and before that Carroll Alley.

## From Cornhill Street to East Street

*45 Fleet Street* is the *Christopher Hohne House* built about 1770 as a residence. It is clapboard, with Flemish bond chimneys and galleted stone foundations, and is one of the nicest examples of the eighteenth-century gambrel-roofed houses in Annapolis. It was built by Andrew Slicer, one of the cabinetmakers who worked on the State House, as a residence. Christopher Hohne and his wife Mary, the daughter of Francis Holland, lived in the house until Hohne's death in 1833. Hohne was once awarded fifty dollars by the legislature for saving the State House dome when it was threatened by fire. He also fought in the Revolution and the War of 1812. After the house passed out of the Hohne family, it belonged to the Revells, the Brewers, and the Tydings.

*16–30 Fleet Street.* These mid-nineteenth-century residences are two stories high and built of clapboard.

*49–50 Fleet Street* are late eighteenth or early nineteenth-century Federal buildings of brick, built as residences.

## East Street

In the early days of the history of Annapolis, East Street extended into the area now occupied by the United States Naval Academy and ended at the governor's house, located on the site of present-day Bancroft Hall.

The original Governor's Mansion was built about 1740 by Edmund Jenings, secretary of the province, on four acres of ground. The building followed the Palladian pattern of a central block flanked by symmetrical hyphens and wings, but it also boasted an unusual semioctagonal entrance bay. Between 1753 and 1769 the house was rented by Horatio Sharpe when he was governor. It was then purchased by Governor Robert Eden in 1769. When Governor Eden returned to England in 1776, the

house was confiscated by the state and used as the Governor's
Mansion until 1866, when the present structure on State Circle
was built. The house was ceded to the Naval Academy, which
used it as a library. Although Ernest Flagg, architect of the Naval
Academy, wished to retain the house as a home for the superintendent, its location conflicted with the symmetry of his overall
plan, and he reluctantly ordered it demolished in 1901. Many of
the gentry visited the Governor's Mansion before and after the
Revolution and traveled up and down East Street to reach it.

   With the exception of the Brice House, the buildings along
East Street were built in the nineteenth century, for the most
part as homes for working people employed in the town.

## From State Circle to King George Street

*91 East Street* was built about 1785 by Captain James West. It was a
two-and-a-half-story gambrel-roofed residence and was altered
in the mid to late nineteenth century for use as a school for African-American children. The school, known as Galilean Hall,
was run by the "Order of the Galilean Fisherman." The school
building was the nineteenth century's oldest continually operated school for black children.

*80–82 East Street* was probably built in the 1730s to 1750s as a
one-and-a-half-story rental unit on property owned by Judge
John Brice. As the east gable-end wall indicates, it was altered to
a full two stories and divided into two dwelling units in the
mid-nineteenth century.

*42 East Street* is the *Brice House,* begun in 1767 by James Brice.
James's father John Brice II lived across Prince George Street in a
small gambrel-roofed house and kept his office in a wing that no
longer stands. *His* father, John Brice I, had acquired the lots on
East Street by 1713. John II began to gather the materials for a
large structure and had actually begun to excavate for the mas-

Brice House, 42 East Street

sive foundations of a new home in 1761, but he got no further. At his death in 1766, John Brice II left the building of the town house to his second son, James Brice, who was then twenty years old.

For the next seven years James Brice kept detailed records of each step in the completion of his thirty-three room mansion. His account book details the cost of the shingles, planks, lathe, hair, stone, bricks, and nails. He lists the names and the wages of each bricklayer, mason, carpenter, joiner, and servant who worked for him during the period of construction. The cost of construction then was 4,014 pounds sterling.

The house is a typical example of the Maryland five-part plan. The kitchen is in the east wing and the carriage house is on the west; these two wings are connected to the central portion of the house by hyphens. The brick is laid in all-header bond and the end chimneys tower ninety feet above the street. The modern roof is of terra-cotta tiles made to look like the original wooden shingles. The walls supporting the high, steeply pitched roof are three feet thick. The interior features a superb mahogany staircase, much decorative plasterwork, and a barrel-vaulted second-story corridor, reputed to be the only one of its kind constructed in eighteenth-century America. The exquisite wood carving in the ballroom is one of the finest features of the Brice House.

James Brice married Juliana Jenings, whose family had purchased the Paca House next door in 1781. It is said he gave her the house as a wedding gift. James Brice served as a member of the governor's council, as mayor of Annapolis in 1782 and again in 1788, as a member of the Maryland Council of Safety, and as a lieutenant in the Anne Arundel County militia. He also served as acting governor of Maryland in 1791–92 after Governor George Plater succumbed to gallstones. With the outbreak of the Revolution, Brice was commissioned as a colonel of the Maryland militia and was thereafter called Colonel Brice. Among the visitors to the Brice House were General George Washington, General Lafayette, General Nathaniel Greene, General John Dickenson, and James Madison. According to Annapolis legend, visitors of the spectral kind have come to the house as well. Over the years occupants of the Brice House have reported sighting a variety of ghosts—James Brice, a nursemaid who feeds resident infants, and a stately young woman who at midnight rests her elbows on the parlor mantelpiece. Thomas Murdock claimed in the nineteenth century that a giant spider attacked him while he was whitewashing the cavernous cellar. Murdock escaped unscathed, but he swore that the spider bit off the handle of his whitewash brush. The Brice House has certainly merited the title of "most haunted house in Annapolis."

James Brice died in 1801. The house remained in the Brice family until 1876, when it was purchased by the Martin family. Thomas E. Martin was elected mayor of Annapolis in 1879. In the 1930s the house was purchased by St. John's College and converted into faculty apartments. In 1953 it was bought by the Wohl family, who restored the house and furnished it with appropriate period pieces. The Brice House was again placed on the market after the death of Stanley Wohl in 1979; it was sold at public auction in 1982 to the International Union of Bricklayers and Allied Craftsmen who are undertaking an extensive renovation.

*Waterwitch Hook and Ladder Station #1* was constructed in 1913. The present Italianate-style building was occupied by the all-volunteer Waterwitch Fire Department until 1986. It was converted to condominiums in 2002.

## PINKNEY STREET

Pinkney Street is one of the earliest business streets in Annapolis. Ashbury Sutton, one of the most important shipbuilders in the eighteenth century, kept a tavern and store and owned a rope-walk on the street. Thomas Flemming, his neighbor, made blocks (for block-and-tackle use). On the City Dock adjacent to Pinkney Street were warehouses and the Ships' Carpenters' Lot, a place set aside for ship construction. The area was busy with the industries important to the maritime development of the town. In the nineteenth century commerce declined, and Pinkney Street began to assume the residential character it retains today. At one point during its long history Pinkney Street was nicknamed Soapsuds Alley, presumably because several residents took in laundry and allowed their used water to drain down the street into the harbor.

## From Market Space to East Street

*4 Pinkney Street* is a restored eighteenth-century warehouse built adjacent to a building that contained a tobacco "prise," which pressed leaf tobacco into the barrels called "hogsheads," the standard eighteenth-century measure, for shipping. Such warehouses would have been typical close to the city dock and this one has been restored by Historic Annapolis Foundation to interpret the tobacco and shipping economy. It now houses a model of the eighteenth-century waterfront town.

*18 Pinkney Street,* the *Shiplap House,* was built in several stages, beginning about 1715 when Edward Smith built the east end. It was enlarged to its present form by a succession of owners in the eighteenth and nineteenth centuries. Smith used the house as his residence and an inn to house "strangers." His guests may have come by sail, ferry, or coach. If business was slow, he could always fall back on his trade—he was a "sawyer," a man who sawed lumber into lengths, in this case probably for the shipbuilders on the Ships' Carpenters' Lot. In his inventory are listed leather-bottom chairs, pewter tankards, small casks of rum, and a lignum vitae punch bowl to prepare punch for his guests, one of the duties of a good innkeeper.

In 1738, Ashbury Sutton, a shipbuilder and ferryman, lived at number 18. Captain Sutton was a substantial property holder. He not only built ships, kept tavern, and ran the ferry, but he also made rope, an important adjunct to his shipbuilding enterprise. In 1748 he sold the house and moved to Prince George's County. When the property was sold, it was listed as consisting of a dwelling house, coach or chaise house, meat house, cook house, and ropewalk.

Sutton's daughter Ann married Samuel Horatio Middleton, who kept tavern next door. He took over Sutton's ferry, which subsequently became known as Middleton's ferry and grew famous during the Revolution for carrying passengers to Rock

Shiplap House Herb Garden, 18 Pinkney Street

Hall on the Eastern Shore. This Bay crossing formed an essential link in the major north-south route in the eighteenth century. Among the users of the ferry was George Washington, who was delayed on a journey to Annapolis when the ferry went aground on Horn Point in a dreadful storm. He wrote that he was damp, forced to sleep in a bunk that was much too short for him, and vastly relieved to get ashore. Tench Tilghman, on his way to Philadelphia with the message of Cornwallis's surrender at Yorktown, crossed the Bay on Middleton's ferry. Thomas Jefferson records in a note that he paid Samuel Middleton passage money to Rock Hall.

Later owners of the house were John Riatt and Nathan Hammond, who imported exotic goods and advertised them for sale: spices, tea, sugar, "spiritous liquors, shallowns and callimancus." Spiritous liquors have not changed, but the reader might not know that "shallowns" refers to woolen fabric used for linings and "callimancus" to a woolen, glossy fabric with a checked pattern only on one side, made in Flanders.

The house was also rented by the cabinetmaker John Shaw about 1765, and in 1787 by John Humphrey, who kept a tavern at the sign of the "Harp and Crown." The Slicer family owned the house for the longest period of time. They lived there from about 1800 until it was bought by Frank Blackwell Mayer in 1880. Mayer was an artist who painted charming watercolor views of Annapolis, recording the street scenes of his day. The old Slicer house was the first and only home owned by Frank Mayer. From his vantage point on Pinkney Street he noted that Annapolis "is full of old architecture and if the powers that be had but the wisdom to preserve them, would become a place of great interest in the future." He said his house was "built long before Annapolis had its street laid out . . . the growth of it having by then turned the house around with windows from which to view on all sides the every varying views of cloud, city, and water."

Throughout Frank Mayer's life in Annapolis, he was concerned about the preservation of the "Ancient City." He decried the "modernization" of the State House, labeling it a "mutilation" and an "act of vandalism." His outrage bore fruit when the State of Maryland restored the Old Senate Chamber in 1902, only about fifteen years after modernizing it. Mayer formed the Local Improvement Association of Annapolis and was vice president of the Anne Arundel County Historical Society.

Mayer received two commissions from the State of Maryland for large paintings to be hung in the State House. One was *Planting the Colony of Maryland,* finished in 1893; the other, *The Burning of the Peggy Stewart,* was finished in 1898. Both still hang in public rooms.

The Shiplap House is wood frame with a steeply pitched roof. The east end with chimney was rebuilt in brick in the mid to late eighteenth century. The one-story frame addition on the west gable end was built about 1817. It is one of the most interesting buildings in Annapolis with its steep roof, tall chimneys, and picturesque medieval appearance. "Shiplap" refers to the way in which the clapboarding is installed. Ashbury Sutton was a shipbuilder, and during his ownership he may have repaired the wooden facade, overlaying the clapboards as he would have done in constructing the hull of a ship.

When Historic Annapolis, Inc., bought the Shiplap House in the 1950s, it had been divided into many small apartments and housed more than twenty people. The building now serves as the headquarters of the Historic Annapolis Foundation.

*29–41 Pinkney Street* are small residences built in the late nineteenth century as homes for working-class people in the town.

*43 Pinkney Street* is called "the Barracks" in commemoration of the fact that troops were housed all over Annapolis during the Revolutionary period. The State of Maryland leased such buildings as this one to house soldiers who were stationed in Annapolis while awaiting reassignment to a battle area. It is a simple gambrel-roofed house built in the early nineteenth century as an artisan's residence.

*51 Pinkney Street* is an example of the American version of English Regency, a style that was popular in the decades from 1790 to 1830.

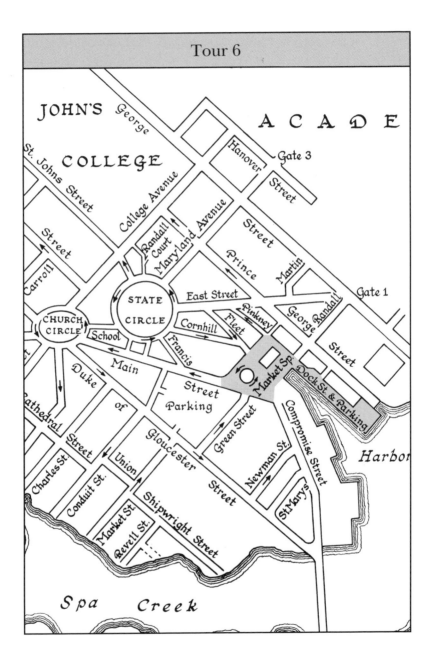

# Market Space and Dock Street

## *MARKET SPACE*

### At the Foot of Main, Cornhill, and Pinkney Streets

From the first shipbuilding and repair operation of Thomas Todd, the seventeenth-century town grew to an area that extended from a line running roughly along the south side of Main Street to a point just below the intersection with Francis Street, straight across to Pinkney Street, and down along the north side of Dock Street. The line of buildings along Market Space today is built on the "Sand Bank" that was formed when the natural sand fill and rubbish collection together began to silt up the waterfront in the early eighteenth century.

The hardware store and small restaurants on the north side of the dock today have replaced the warehouses and shipbuilding operations located there in the eighteenth century. The goods from ships were unloaded and stored until they were sold and either delivered to local merchants or shipped on to plantation owners and even merchants in other areas served by the port of Annapolis. Warehouses also occupied the opposite side of the dock along lower Main Street. In 1770 Charles Carroll, the Barrister, had a wharf at the foot of what is now Green Street. About the same time, the Ships' Carpenters' Lot, a public place for the construction of ships, was specifically designated on the north side of the dock. Also located on the point on the north side of the dock was the battery with its cannon, which never had to be fired in defense of the settlement but was used to salute the Crown or the governor. Annapolitans unsuccessfully attempted to use this cannon against rowdy

Baltimoreans during the 1847 riot at the dock involving the steamship *Jewess.*

In 1770 a number of buildings used by the representatives of British merchants lined the head of the dock. These representatives, called factors, made arrangements for the shipment of the planters' produce to England and Scotland in exchange for much desired British goods. In 1883 a fire almost destroyed the whole of "Factors Row" between Main and Cornhill Streets. The buildings standing today were constructed after the fire on the surviving eighteenth-century foundations, one of which may still be seen in the northeast wall of number *26 Market Space.* A building erected by Charles Wallace, the developer of Cornhill and Pinkney Streets, was among those destroyed.

*8 Market Space* was erected in the late nineteenth century. The northwest addition is a new building, constructed in the form of an early warehouse.

*2 Market Space, Middleton's Tavern,* was probably built about 1754, several years after Samuel Horatio Middleton purchased the property from Elizabeth Bennett in 1750. The Bennetts had also kept a tavern there. Middleton called his establishment an "Inn for Sea Faring Men." He also took over his father-in-law's ferry, re-named it Middleton's Ferry, and carried passengers, carriages, wagons, and goods across the Bay to Rock Hall. Samuel Middleton kept a store in a portion of the building, ran an import business, and built ships on the tavern lot as well. He died in 1770.

Middleton's Tavern was one of the outstanding places to visit in Annapolis. It was used by members of the Continental Congress as well as members of the Maryland Jockey Club, the Free Masons, and the Tuesday Club. It was probably the place where President James Monroe was entertained when he visited Annapolis in 1818. The tavern was owned then by John Randall, who was mayor of Annapolis. Randall, a logistics officer during the Revolution, was ward to William Buckland, the architect of the Hammond-Harwood House. The building has been greatly changed on the interior over the years as the result of fire. Following the fire in 1970, the exterior was restored and the building placed under a preservation easement. The activities that flourish inside are much the same as they were in the eighteenth century—drinking, dining, and conversation.

## DOCK STREET

### From Randall Street to the City Dock

*126 and 142 Dock Street* are two twentieth-century buildings that function as hardware stores or "ship's chandleries" today. They are built on the site of the eighteenth-century Ships' Carpenters' Lot.

*132 and 136 Dock Street* are late eighteenth and early nineteenth-century structures. The building at number 136 Dock Street has a wall of exposed stone that is said to have been part of the City Jail. At one time the jail was said to be in the area of the City Gate (at West and Cathedral Streets today); at a later date, it was located near the dock. Many references to the poor conditions of the jail were reported in the *Maryland Gazette* of the day. About 1740 the jail was pulled down, and the stones were used in another building.

Other buildings along Dock Street were built in the twentieth century, including a grocery store that was converted to a shopping mall and a restaurant complex. In the center of the large municipal parking lot is the present *Harbor Master's Building*. From this building an officer of the city government directs activities along the city's docking facility.

*John Inch's Shop* was located on "Southeast Street on the Point near the guns." He advertised in the *Maryland Gazette* in 1749

Market Space and City Dock

that he had set up business as a goldsmith. He would do gold and silver work and would clean and mend clocks and watches. A little later he advertised in the *Gazette* that he had a license and "keeps good entertainment for Man and Horse." He also kept a boat to carry passengers to "Kent-Island and Eastern-Neck." In 1758 he advertised that he sold lemons, and in 1759, he made "enamel Rings for Mourning." He ran a tannery at the same address, as well as a store where he sold guns, wine, oil, vinegar, and codfish, among other items in demand in the town. John

Inch obviously was determined to succeed at one or another of his many enterprises.

## City Market House

*Market House* stands in the center of Market Square. The current Market House, constructed in 1858, is the third structure built on the site. In 1784 eight prominent Annapolis businessmen donated the land to the city, declaring that the site was to be utilized only as a city market. The current structure, although simple in style, was built with cast-iron frames and covered with a West Indian–style roof. In 1968, the building was slated by the City Council for demolition as part of a waterfront renovation project. However, widespread public disapproval and a "Save the Market House" campaign convinced the council in 1969 to reverse its decision and to restore the Market House instead.

In 1717 market was held in the open on Mondays and Wednesdays "under the flagg staffe on State House hill," and the town drummer beat the drum to give notice. Some time after 1717 a market house was erected in State Circle; the site was later occupied by the State Land Record Office, which stood at the head of Maryland Avenue until the early twentieth century.

In 1728 the Maryland Assembly passed an act that provided land for a new market house at the foot of Church Street (now Main). The city erected a building to house the market, but it never seemed to catch on in the new location and was not much used. In 1751 the market house and lot were sold to Lancelot Jacques, and in 1752 the market was again held on State House Hill at Maryland Avenue. The market building at the foot of Main Street was eventually washed away in September 1774 by the same hurricane that blew off the newly installed roof of the State House.

*The traffic circle* at the intersection of Main and Compromise streets was laid out in 1885 in a spirit of civic improvement. Planners envisioned a green park dominated by an equestrian statue, the subject of which remained to be decided. No statue was forthcoming, however, and the park languished. In 1908 public spirit was aroused again when Annapolitans decided to erect a monument in the circle to commemorate the two hundredth anniversary of the grant of the city charter. Baltimore architects designed an imposing fountain surmounted by a statue of Cecilius Calvert extending religious toleration to figures representing Catholics, Anglicans, and Puritans. The city government, however, failed to raise the funds needed for this ambitious undertaking. Although a cornerstone, replete with time capsule, was laid in November 1908, the remainder of the fountain complex failed to materialize. The time capsule has since disappeared, but the cornerstone survives as part of the Market House park.

A gas station was built on the circle after World War I. With the restoration of the harbor in the 1960s and 1970s the gas station was demolished, and the circle once again was converted to a park. Seasonal plantings and a flagpole that flies the city flag now fulfill the original dream of a park.

Located at City Dock, the Kunta Kinte–Alex Haley Memorial commemorates the place where Haley's ancestor, the enslaved Kunta Kinte, landed in America, according to Haley's book *Roots*. This unique memorial features a life-size sculpture grouping by Ed Dwight showing Haley reading to three children, a story wall with bronze plaques quoting the author's writings, and a compass rose made of bronze and multicolored granite. A seating area overlooks the harbor where *Lord Ligonier*, the ship that carried Kunta Kinte, docked.

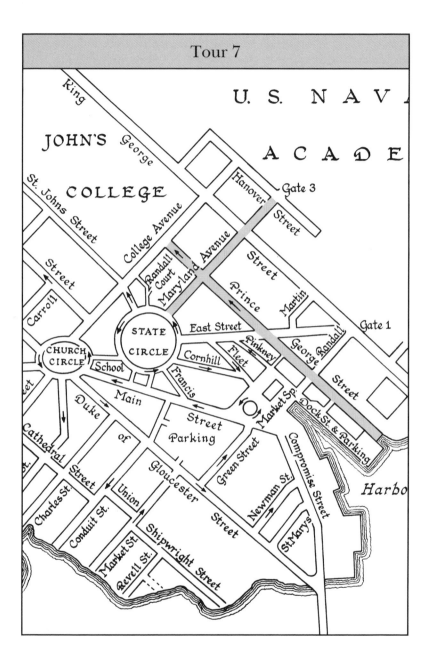

U. S. N A V A

A C A D E

JOHN'S

COLLEGE

King George

Gate 3

St. Johns Street

College Avenue

Hanover Street

Street

Street

Randall Court

Maryland Avenue

Prince

Martin

Carroll

STATE CIRCLE

East Street

Gate 1

CHURCH CIRCLE

School

Cornhill

Pinkney

Fleet

George

Randall

Street

Francis

Main

Market Sp.

Dock St. & Parking

Duke

of

Street Parking

Green Street

Compromise Street

Harbo

Cathedral Street

Union St.

Gloucester Street

Newman St.

Charles St.

Conduit St.

St Marys

Market St.

Revell St.

Shipwright Street

# Maryland Avenue, Cumberland Court, and Prince George Street

## *MARYLAND AVENUE*

In the eighteenth century, Maryland Avenue—then called Northeast Street—ran to the water. It was nicknamed the "Patriots Walk" because many members of the Continental Congress and other influential Annapolitans involved in "federal business" lived along the street. Thomas Jefferson and James Madison rented a residence owned by Daniel Dulany and passed down this street each day. The Dulany House, in the area where Bancroft Hall is located today, was used as a residence by superintendents of the Naval Academy from 1845 until it was demolished in 1883. Samuel Chase and Mathias Hammond also chose this street for their great homes in the years before the Revolution. In the late nineteenth century, Maryland Avenue assumed the commercial character it still bears today. Midshipmen who patronized the many tailor shops and novelty stores that dotted the street until World War II gave it the nickname "Robber's Row."

### From the Naval Academy (Gate 3) to State Circle

*5 Maryland Avenue,* built sometime between 1878 and 1900, is a stuccoed Italianate villa with a spired belvedere. With its conversion into apartments in the twentieth century, the house suffered several badly designed additions. It has recently been renovated.

*8 Maryland Avenue,* built in 1857 as a Victorian rental property, is still an apartment building today.

*9–11 Maryland Avenue* is called the *Tilton House* after a previous owner. Built about 1760 by Thomas Rutland, who also built the Peggy Stewart House, this house is a two-story brick dwelling with four bays. It displays many characteristics of eighteenth-century Annapolis buildings: massive end chimneys, a high stone foundation with galleting, a simple water table, and a front elevation laid in header bond. Colonel Edward Tilton traveled with Admiral Perry to Japan and had a distinguished career in the Marine Corps.

*12 Maryland Avenue* was built in 1894 by Hope Day Schouler as a single-family house and reflects the transition from shingle style to Colonial Revival. It was converted to apartments in 1948.

*15 Maryland Avenue* represents a subdued version of the Italianate style. It was constructed in 1860 for Dr. Thomas O. Walton and remained in the family for over one hundred years.

*16 Maryland Avenue* was built about 1852 to 1858 for James Andrew, an Irish immigrant and Main Street merchant, on land that was once part of the Hammond-Harwood property. It is one of the few dwellings built in the Greek Revival style in Annapolis.

*19 Maryland Avenue,* the *Hammond-Harwood House,* was begun in 1774 by William Buckland for Mathias Hammond. Hammond was a young plantation owner whose recent election to the provincial legislature, as well as his interest in the Revolutionary movement, made it advantageous to have a house in town. The lot on which the house was built, four acres in extent, stretched from King George Street on the north to Prince George Street on the south and to William Paca's wall on the east. One of the largest single holdings in the town, it was called Hammond's Square.

The building has been described as one of the finest classical dwellings in America. The five-part plan includes two half-octagonal wings flanking the center block and connected to it with hyphens. The central section is divided into five bays, with two windows on either side of the double door. This double door, with its elaborately carved spandrel of fruits and flowers, has been justly called one of the most beautiful entranceways in America. The wings were designed as service buildings, that on the south as the kitchen and that on the north a law office. The hyphens were the service (or "foul weather") entrances. The central block contains eight rooms, most designed for formal entertainment.

The interior of the Hammond-Harwood House is in the main original. The halls are wainscoted to the chair rails and the chair rails, skirt boards, and door and window frames are all carved wood. The beautiful cornices are molded plaster.

The symmetry of the house extends to the smallest details. Some of the doors are false—they were carved merely to balance other functioning doors. The dining room is another example of the architect's determination to achieve perfect balance. Although the rear wall appears to have three windows, one of those windows is really a door. In this jib door the lower sash raises up into the upper frame, the bolt on the paneling below pulls back, and the resulting door leads to the garden. The rear of the house echoes the front in its five bays, but here the windows are set off by giant brick pilasters. During construction, William Buckland died, and Mathias Hammond assumed direction of the workmen. Although the house was completed by 1776, for some unknown reason Hammond never lived in it. He rented the house in 1784 when Annapolis was the capital of the United States, and he continued to own the house until his death. Mathias Hammond willed the house to his nephews, who also failed to occupy it. They sold it in 1810 to Ninian Pinkney, Sr., who lived there for about a year. He in turn sold the house to Judge Jeremiah Townley Chase in 1811. Judge Chase gave the house to his daughter Frances Townley Chase Loockerman, who lived there with her family until her death in 1857. It was

Hammond-Harwood
House, 19 Maryland
Avenue

inherited by her daughter, Hester Anne Loockerman Harwood,
wife of William Harwood. Hester Anne in turn left the house to
her daughter, also named Hester Anne, who never married and
died without a will in 1924. The family heirlooms and the house
itself then were sold at public auction.

Among the pieces sold at auction were paintings by Charles Willson Peale of the ancestors of William Harwood, including one of William Buckland, who was Harwood's great-great-grandfather.

The house was bought by St. John's College, which operated it as a museum for five years. The interior was furnished with pieces from the Mabel Garvan Collection at Yale University, some of which the Garvan family had acquired at the Harwood sale. With the onset of the Depression, St. John's could no longer afford to operate the museum. After standing empty and shuttered for several years, the house was sold in 1940 to the newly formed Hammond-Harwood House Association, which continues to operate it today as a house museum.

*22 Maryland Avenue* is the *Chase-Lloyd House.* Samuel Chase was born on the Eastern Shore, the son of the rector of a parish in Somerset County. He came to Annapolis in 1759 at the age of eighteen to study law under John Hammond and John Hall. Two years later he was admitted to the bar. He became known for his fiery oratory.

His political stance made more enemies than friends for Chase. He seemed always to place himself in opposition to the governor. He took a strong stand against "taxation without representation" as embodied in the Stamp Act, and he became involved in a controversy over the sale of overpriced flour to the Continental Army in 1778. At that time Chase was forced to resign from the Continental Congress. He had previously been active in other capacities for the American government. In 1775 he was sent to Canada with a delegation made up of Benjamin Franklin, Charles Carroll, and John Carroll to win the support of the Canadian people in the cause of freedom. The mission failed due to the suspicions of the Catholic French Canadians concerning the American commitment to religious toleration.

In 1796 Chase was appointed a justice of the Supreme Court of the United States by President Washington. He was impeached over a scandal during Jefferson's administration but was eventually acquitted.

Samuel Chase married Anne Baldwin in 1762, and they made great plans for a fine new house in Annapolis on which construction began in 1769. By 1771 Chase realized that he could not afford to complete his ambitious plans, and he sold the unfinished house to Edward Lloyd IV of Wye Plantation on

Chase-Lloyd House, 22 Maryland Avenue

the Eastern Shore. "Edward the Magnificent," as he was called, was extremely wealthy and lived in a manner that can only be described as opulent. When he came across the Bay to his residence in Annapolis by barge, he was rowed by liveried servants. The barge itself sported portholes framed by decorative cartouches designed by the architect William Buckland.

The interior detail of the house on Maryland Avenue was completed by William Buckland, who had worked on the Virginia home of Anne Tayloe Lloyd, Edward's wife. Lloyd kept detailed account books listing the names of his architect and craftsmen during the two and a half years it took to complete the structure to his satisfaction. The cantilevered main stairway frames a great Palladian window, and the carved moldings and cornices are festooned with ribbons, grapes, roses, and elaborate classical motifs. In the front parlor of the house, Mary Tayloe Lloyd, the youngest daughter of Edward IV, married Francis Scott Key in 1802. In 1809 Edward Lloyd V, the eldest son, became governor of Maryland.

After seventy-three years in the hands of the Lloyds and their descendants, the house was sold to Hester Anne Chase, the daughter of Jeremiah Townley Chase. She lived there until her death in 1875, when the house passed into the hands of her three nieces. The last surviving niece, the wife of Samuel Ridout, died in 1886 and bequeathed the house to a board of twelve members, the president to be the bishop of the Episcopal Diocese of Maryland, for the purpose of operating the house as a home for elderly ladies "where they may find a retreat from the vicissitudes of life." The foundation was to be called the Chase Home and is so known today.

*30 Maryland Avenue* was built between 1891 and 1903. The house is an excellent example of the Queen Anne style. It is the only structure on the block constructed in this style that has retained its original design and ornamentation.

*29–31 Maryland Avenue* is a commercial building built in the Italianate style around 1860. This building and its immediate neighbor, number 33–35, have elaborate cornices.

*32 Maryland Avenue* is probably the best example of French Second Empire architecture in Annapolis. It was built about 1879 by John H. Thomas, mayor of Annapolis from 1893 to 1897, and is a fine, large, well-constructed building. The finished brick and thin "butter joints" of the facade provide an observable contrast with the rougher brickwork of the sides.

*33–35 Maryland Avenue* is nearly identical to its neighbor at 29–31 Maryland Avenue. It was built as a commercial building and is still used as such today.

*36 Maryland Avenue* is a post–Civil War town house. The dwelling is a good example of the Italianate style of architecture.

*38 Maryland Avenue* was designed in the Second Empire style. The dwelling is an imposing frame structure topped by a substantial mansard roof, and it features a prominent corner tower. Built in 1877, the structure was not the first one on the site. Stables belonging to the Lloyd family stood on the site until 1846, when they were demolished and the brick used to construct the First Presbyterian Church on Duke of Gloucester Street.

*44 Maryland Avenue* was the Masonic Lodge and the Annapolis Opera House. The building was constructed in 1872 in the Italianate style to be used as a Masonic meeting hall, opera house, or store. Decorating the keystones of the second-story windows are the nine Masonic symbols, and the cornerstone on the Maryland Avenue facade is dated. "Opera" in Annapolis in 1872 was not the classic sort, but rather shows by Annie Oakley and Buffalo Bill Cody. The hall also served as a Naval Academy preparatory school. It is now occupied by shops on the street level and by offices above.

*49 Maryland Avenue* was constructed between 1823 and 1844 in the Federal style. The dwelling was converted from residentia1 to commercial between 1930 and 1954.

*55–57 Maryland Avenue* was built between 1911 and 1913 as a commercial/residential building.

*56 Maryland Avenue* was built in the mid to late nineteenth century as a commercial brick structure. In the late 1980s the building collapsed on itself, like a house of cards. It was sympathetically rebuilt.

*67–69 Maryland Avenue* was constructed between 1897 and 1903 in a Classical Revival style with Adamesque detailing. The history of the property illustrates the development of the only iron-fronted building on Maryland Avenue.

*75 Maryland Avenue* is a Victorian commercial building erected about 1870.

*Maryland Avenue and State Circle.* This corner building is a Greek Revival style, temple-front building, constructed in 1845. In 1878 it was the headquarters of the Annapolis Sons of Temperance; by 1908 it had passed to the YMCA. After World War I it was converted into a retail establishment.

## CUMBERLAND COURT

### Off Maryland Avenue between Prince George and King George Streets

*Cumberland Court* is one of those delightful, hidden cul-de-sacs that abound in Annapolis. It is a small, private street of seven houses that runs from Maryland Avenue to the wall of William Paca's garden. This parcel of land, the last to be extracted from Mathias

Hammond's four-acre tract, was sold by Hester Anne Harwood in 1907 shortly after the death of her sister Lucy. The property was developed immediately thereafter. Some of the houses are quite modern, though others are of the period of the early 1900s.

*The Annapolis Ferry* was a ferry system that crossed the Severn River from Annapolis to the Broadneck Peninsula and operated from the landing at the end of Northeast Street, now Maryland Avenue. The ferry served the area until 1887 when the first bridge over the river was built.

The ferryman in 1695 was Allen Robnett, who was required to live in Annapolis. He was paid nine thousand pounds of tobacco a year out of public revenues. The ferry and the landings were maintained by the county until 1887.

## PRINCE GEORGE STREET

Prince George Street, laid out in 1695, was named after George of Denmark, the husband of the future Queen Anne. In 1718 King George and Prince George Streets extended only as far as Randall Street, at that time the site of a tidal inlet called the Governor's Pond.

## From Spa Creek to College Avenue

*110 Prince George Street* is the *MacCubbin-Paterson House*. Built in the eighteenth century and modified in the nineteenth century, it is located in the waterfront area called "Wapping Street" in the early days. The district undoubtedly received its name from the many English sailors familiar with the dock area of that name east of London. The lots on the water were first owned by Patrick Creagh, and later in 1760 by Richard MacCubbin, a businessman and tobacco plantation owner, who built his fine house about 1786.

A peek around the side of the house will provide a glimpse of the original eighteenth-century walls.

*130 Prince George Street,* the *Sands House,* was built on property owned by Evan Jones, who kept a tavern and served as an alderman of the city. Although Jones held several other posts such as deputy collector of customs and assistant clerk of the assembly, he was constantly in debt and in 1706 mortgaged his house to Dr. Charles Carroll. At Jones's death, his wife and son deeded the title in full to Dr. Charles Carroll. The lot was divided into three portions and sold by Dr. Carroll. The eastern section was leased to Joseph Evitts, a joiner, who later bought the property. In 1757 Evitts's daughter Martha married Thomas Brooks Hodgkin, a merchant. Three years later Hodgkin bought the house from his father-in-law. In 1768 Hodgkin sold the house to John Carty, a shipwright, who sold it in turn to John Sands, a mariner and sailmaker. Sands died in 1791, and the property passed into the hands of the children. It has continued to descend in the family for five generations. The house is an eighteenth-century frame dwelling with clapboard siding. The original gambrel-roofed house was soon altered, encapsulating the original roof with round-butt shingles secured by hand-wrought nails. The setting of the house has also changed. It originally overlooked Governor's Pond, but because of subsequent silting and filling, it is now located a block from City Dock.

*134 Prince George Street* is an early twentieth-century Georgian Revival structure. The garden fence, in the "star and anchor" pattern, was retrieved from the Naval Academy when Ernest Flagg replaced the fencing that ran along King George Street with the brick wall that stands there today.

*142–144 Prince George Street* was originally a center passage Georgian residence built between 1783 and 1785 of brick, but later covered with stucco. It was originally a five-bay structure with

Sands House, 130 Prince George Street

huge end chimneys and elliptical roof dormers. A tunnel that leads from the basement of number 144 toward the harbor has long been celebrated as a passageway used by smugglers to transport embargoed goods. In fact, the tunnel was probably a hypocaust, a passage used to convey heat from an underground stove.

The most prominent owner of the house in the eighteenth century was Dr. James Murray, a physician and patriot during the Revolution. The family later gave its name to the Murray Hill neighborhood off West Street. About 1845 James Iglehart purchased number 142 from the Murray estate. His daughter

Anne Sellman Iglehart became the wife of Captain James Waddell, who built number 61 College Avenue in 1868 (see the description of the house with tour 1). After the Civil War number 142 passed to the Werntz family, who operated the Naval Academy Preparatory School in the Masonic meeting hall on Maryland Avenue until 1937 (see tour 7, 44 Maryland Avenue).

The northwestern part of the building, number 144, is an early nineteenth-century addition that adds an unsymmetrical sixth bay to the facade. The eighteenth-century chimney marking the original end of the house can still be discerned jutting through the roof.

*160 Prince George Street* was owned by Patrick Creagh, the "undertaker," shipbuilder, and supplier of building materials. The house is a good example of a small, freestanding, mid-eighteenth-century dwelling occupied by a successful Annapolis artisan and tradesman. Creagh was also a painter, farmer, craftsman, shipowner, mariner, tobacco merchant, and brewer. Later the house was owned by the free African-American couple, John and Lucy Smith. Smith was a "drayer" or hauler who also operated a livery stable in the rear of the property. His wife operated Aunt Lucy's bakeshop at the corner of Main and Green Streets.

*162 Prince George Street* was erected between 1878 and 1886 as a chapel of ease for St. Anne's Church. In 1918 St. Anne's sold the building to Kneseth Israel Synagogue, which occupied it until 1962. Professor Marshal Oliver designed the building and this is his only know architectural design. It is a fine example of late nineteenth century Gothic-influenced ecclesiastical design and a successful application of a rich array of architectural detail to a compact building on a somewhat challenging site.

*182 Prince George Street* is a Victorian town house built sometime after 1885 as a residence.

*185 Prince George Street* is a finely proportioned residence in the Victorian style built about 1860.

*186 Prince George Street* is the *William Paca House.* William Paca began his great house in 1763. He was a young attorney from Harford County who had studied law in Annapolis with Stephen Bordley. In 1763 Paca married Mary Chew and four days after their wedding he bought two lots on Prince George Street for their home. It took about two years to complete the house, which was the first of the five-part-plan houses built in Annapolis. The exterior of the building is of brick with very simple decoration on the cornices and window and doorframes. It has a steeply pitched roof, a reminder of medieval buildings, but all of the door and window openings are evenly placed. The large brick chimneys at each end of the central section give it the appearance of even greater height.

The house contains thirty-seven rooms. Thirteen of these rooms, including hallways, are open to visitors and are furnished in the manner of the period. Much research went into the restoration of the woodwork, plastering, and paint colors. The house was used as a family residence, and though the exterior design is severely formal, the interior rooms are not necessarily symmetrical. Household inventories of Paca family members and of other individuals of similar status in the area were used to recreate the interior decor since Paca himself left no record of his furnishings.

William Paca's wife Mary died in 1774, the year Paca began serving as a delegate to the Continental Congress in Philadelphia. In 1780 Paca sold his great house to Thomas Jennings, an attorney.

The Jennings family lived in the house until 1796 when Jennings died, and the family moved. After the Jennings family, the house had many tenants, one of whom was Henri Joseph Stier, a Belgian emigre and owner of one of the most important collections of European art in America. In 1901 the

William Paca House,
186 Prince George Street

house was sold to the Security Land Company, which built a two-hundred-room hotel on the garden site and used the house as the front lobby. The hotel was called Carvel Hall Hotel after the best-selling novel about colonial Annapolis written by Winston Churchill, a cousin of the British prime minister. The elegant hotel served as a social center for the community

and Carvel Hall was popular among visitors to the legislature and the Naval Academy.

In 1965 Carvel Hall Hotel was torn down and the Paca House itself threatened with demolition until Historic Annapolis bought the site and began restoration of both the house and garden. The garden was opened to the public in 1973 and the house in 1976. The summer house in the garden, which sports a statue of Mercury on its pinnacle, was reconstructed on the basis of archaeological remains and its depiction in Charles Willson Peale's portrait of Paca. The garden boasts a fine collection of herbs and antique roses.

*194 Prince George Street* is called the *Gassaway-Feldmeyer House.* Built between 1870 and 1880 as an elegant Italianate residence, it was the Feldmeyer family home for many years. Having been used for offices at one time, it is now a private residence.

*195 Prince George Street* was built around 1739 by Judge John Brice, Jr. In 1760 he bequeathed his lots on East Street to his second son, James, with some building materials to construct the great Brice House (see tour 5, 42 East Street). The Brices must have been extremely attached to their Prince George Street home, since they reproduced its floor plan exactly in the new residence despite the disparity in size. The plan, referred to as the "Annapolis plan," is a modified version of the Georgian plan with a circular rather than axial circulation pattern. The *Little Brice House,* as it is sometimes called, is built of brick with double end chimneys. John Brice's office was in a wing facing toward the water, but it no longer stands.

*196 Prince George Street* was built by Joseph S. M. Basil, who subdivided the property and erected two almost identical dwellings. The structure retains much of its original exterior and interior detailing and stands along with 198 Prince George Street as an excellent example of the Queen Anne style of architecture.

*201 Prince George Street* is called the *Stockett House* for the family that acquired it about 1870 and whose descendants occupied the house until 1984. The house is Colonial Revival in style.

*203 Prince George Street* presents a unique and uncharacteristic facade to the street. Although the building's overall form and mass-

William Paca House Garden

ing cannot be directly associated with any given style, its exterior and interior detailing is twentieth-century Colonial Revival.

*204–208 Prince George Street* is a row of Victorian residences built about 1870. They are of brick and form a delightful visual block on the streetscape. The row is in reality a single building divided into three houses.

*211 Prince George Street,* the *Marchand-Dorsey House,* was built about 1766 by John Brice III, brother of James. It is a Georgian-style house and features a semicircular stairway leading to the front door. The three-story Italianate "tower" on the southeast was added in the nineteenth century.

*222 Prince George Street* was erected in 1870 as the Wesley Chapel by a group from the congregation of Calvary Methodist Church (formerly at the corner of North Street and State Circle). In 1921, Wesley Chapel was converted into a recreation hall. By 1939 the building was occupied by the State Division of Income Taxes. Between 1941 and 1943 it functioned as a USO facility—the United Service Organization provided social and recreational services to members of the armed forces. The old chapel was restored to its original religious purpose, however, when it was purchased by the First Church of Christ Scientist in 1943.

The history of Christian Science in Annapolis goes back to 1909 when a small group began to meet at the home of a naval officer and his wife. In 1914 this group gained official recognition as a society and in 1929 as a church. The church began to meet in 1937 at number 124 College Avenue but soon after sold the property to the state for the construction of the James Office Building. When the First Church moved to 222 Prince George Street the tenant of the building at that time was, ironically, the State Department of Health. The second floor of the building was restored in 1951 and the first floor in 1963. The church was officially dedicated in 1957. The building is a Victorian Gothic

Revival style that recalls architectural massing and details from pre-Gothic to late Gothic. The stumplike steeple has an unfinished look; possibly the congregation planned a more impressive spire but, as was often the case, never got around to building it. Some of the original stained glass has survived, but the first-story windows were presumably bricked up during the period when the church served nonreligious functions. The Christian Science church moved out in 1998 and the building was used for offices that same year. In 2001, it was purchased and developed as three apartments, a project that took two years to complete.

*232–248 Prince George Street* are residences typical of urban design in the 1870s. They are Victorian in style and may have been constructed by the same builder who constructed number 137 Charles Street, number 194 Prince George Street, and numbers 32 and 36 Maryland Avenue.

*243 Prince George Street* is a late nineteenth-century residence in the high Victorian style.

*250 Prince George Street* is a nineteenth-century Victorian residence with Federal trim.

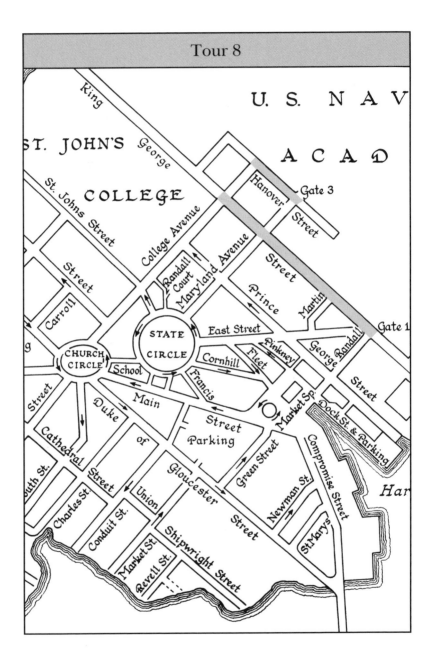

## Tour 8

# King George and Hanover Streets, and the United States Naval Academy

## *KING GEORGE STREET*

King George Street is named after King George I, who succeeded Queen Anne on the British throne in 1714. The area
now behind the Naval Academy wall along the northeast side of
this street was part of the city of Annapolis in the early days. Governor Eden lived there after he bought the Edmund Jenings
house. Thomas Jefferson and James Madison lived at Daniel
Dulany's house in that area. The neighborhood was also the site
of at least one industry, a tannery, operated by Frederick Wolfe
in the 1750s. The ferry to the Eastern Shore left from this location from early days to 1944.

### From the Naval Academy (Gate 1) to College Avenue

*21 King George Street* is a late Victorian residence that abuts number 204 Prince George Street at the rear. Those two lots share an
interesting puzzle. Number 204 Prince George Street has on the
back of its lot some early eighteenth-century walls that may be
the remains of an orangery (greenhouse) and hypocaust. The
lot was bought by William Emerson in 1718 and sold to Charles
Carroll, the Chirurgeon (surgeon), in 1720 for 2 pounds, 8 shillings. In 1747 the elder Daniel Dulany bought the lot for 450
pounds in the name of Alexander Hamilton and his wife, Dulany's
daughter. The increase in the value of the property is attributable
both to the rise in prices and to the houses and garden that by
then, according to the deed, graced the lot. Nothing more specific is known of these structures, which are now covered by late

nineteenth-century dwellings. Under a frame outbuilding at the rear of number 204 Prince George Street is a brick floor, under which were found artifacts dating between 1800 and 1850. These artifacts suggest that a family with children lived in the house about 1830. They probably were connected in some way with the maritime industry and were not prosperous. Hypocausts, or brick heating tunnels, can be found at Mount Vernon and also at Wye House on the Eastern Shore. Such a heating system was planned for the State House in 1768, and the brick walls at number 204 Prince George may be the ruins of an earlier version.

*235 King George Street* is the kitchen of the Chase-Lloyd House (see the description of the house in tour 7). It was built in the Federal style in the early nineteenth century around a large central hooded chimney, a feature that betrays its long use as a kitchen. It is now a residence.

*248 King George Street* is the *Steele House,* constructed prior to 1858 in the Italianate style. It is a fine brick residence. The house belonged to Henry Maynadier Steele, who married Maria Key, the daughter of Francis Scott Key and Mary Tayloe Lloyd.

## *HANOVER STREET*

Hanover Street is named after the House of Hanover, which assumed the British throne upon the death of the Stuart Queen Anne in 1714.

### From the Naval Academy (Gate 3) to College Avenue

*201 Hanover Street* is a mid-nineteenth-century Italianate dwelling. The unadorned cornice and off-white stucco produce an effect of elegant simplicity.

*207 Hanover Street,* the *Peggy Stewart House,* was built by Thomas Rutland between 1761 and 1764. It was leased to William Thomas soon after completion and bought by Daniel of St. Thomas Jenifer in 1772. That same year, Jenifer sold the house to Anthony Stewart, a local merchant and importer.

During Stewart's ownership the *Peggy Stewart* Tea Party took place. The period of the Revolution was one of great unrest in Annapolis. Anthony Stewart's ship *Peggy Stewart* arrived from England with a load which included taxable tea. When Stewart paid the duty on the cargo, the trouble began. The Non-Importation Act had been signed in Maryland, and the Sons of Liberty rioted in front of Stewart's house in protest. They threatened to burn him in effigy, to burn his warehouses, and to destroy his business. Stewart claimed that he knew nothing of the tea shipment, that it was included without his knowledge by his London agent, and that he had paid the duty on the entire cargo so that several ailing sailors could disembark to receive treatment. He also stated that he was not a Tory. Mathias Hammond was able to gain control of the crowd and effect a compromise. The arrangement called for Stewart's brig *(Peggy Stewart)* to be run aground on Windmill Point at what was then the end of Hanover Street and burned to the waterline.

Anthony Stewart felt that he had no future in Annapolis and feared for his life, so he departed for Nova Scotia. Stewart's wife stayed in Annapolis with the children until she was able to make arrangements to dissolve the business enterprises and dispose of the house, which was sold back to Daniel of St. Thomas Jenifer in 1779.

That same year Jenifer again sold the house, this time to Thomas Stone, who was one of the four Maryland signers of the Declaration of Independence. Stone died in 1783, and his heirs sold the house to William Harwood. His son, General Richard Harwood, inherited the property and lived there with his wife, Sarah Callahan, granddaughter of William Buckland.

Peggy Stewart House, 207 Hanover Street

When General Harwood died, the house was put on the market, and advertised in the *Maryland Gazette* in 1837 as "12 spacious rooms, 8 fireplaces, dry cellars, newly painted, 5 acres of grounds, a carriage house, smoke house, dairy, wash house, an excellent pump, a garden planted with choice fruit and shrubbery, all in excellent repair."

Robert Welsh bought the house, and his son Charles inherited the lot. Other residences along Hanover Street began to appear when the land was subdivided.

*215–217 Hanover Street* was the rectory of St. Anne's Episcopal Parish. The lot was conveyed to the church in 1759 by Philip Key and served as the rectory for 116 years. The brick dwelling was built about 1769 and altered between 1897 and 1903 by the addition of a mansard roof. The building is laid in all-header bond on a stone foundation with end chimneys.

Hanover Street was the location of an even earlier rectory. On the corner of Northeast (now Maryland Avenue) and Hanover Street once stood an early building used by Cesar Ghiselin, a silversmith. Born of a French Huguenot family that emigrated from Rouen to London, Ghiselin was working in Philadelphia as early as 1708, and he continued to work there until 1716. He is believed to have moved to Annapolis at that time, but the first record of him in the city is 1718. The first silversmith known to have worked in Annapolis, Ghiselin was commissioned on September 6, 1721, by "the Mayor, Recorder Alderman, and Common Councilmen of Annapolis" to make twelve silver spoons as prizes for a horse race to be run on September 29. Eight of the spoons were awarded to the victor and four to the second horse.

When Ghiselin moved back to Philadelphia in 1729, the property was sold to Ralph Smith. In 1734 it was sold by John Lomas, an "inn holder," and his wife Margaret to the Reverend John Humphrey for 140 pounds sterling. That sum indicates that considerable improvements had been made to the property. Humphrey was the rector at St. Anne's.

After the death of Humphrey, his wife Theodosia married Philip Key. Through the Key family line, Theodosia Humphrey Key was grandmother of Philip Barton Key, the famous Maryland attorney, and John Ross Key, who is the ancestor of Francis Scott Key.

After Philip Key conveyed the Hanover Street property to St. Anne's, the rectory on the corner was demolished and a new structure erected next door at number 215–217 by 1768. The most famous resident of number 215–217 was the Reverend

Jonathan Boucher, a wit who was the rector of St. Anne's in the years just prior to the Revolution. Boucher's entertaining diaries provide one of the best surviving records of life in Annapolis during its most prosperous period. Boucher tutored George Washington's stepson, John Parke Custis, and Washington slept at number 215–217 on more than one occasion.

*219 Hanover Street* is called the *Admiral Apartments*. The building was erected in 1868 in the Italianate style.

*237 Hanover Street* was built in 1835 and is a residence in the Greek Revival style.

*239–241 Hanover Street* is an early nineteenth-century Federal-style double house.

## THE UNITED STATES NAVAL ACADEMY

The U.S. Naval Academy was founded on the site of the army's Fort Severn in 1845. The fort had been established shortly before the War of 1812 to protect the water approaches to the Maryland state capital. The point of land on which the old fort was located was a good vantage point. When the fort was transferred to the Navy Department, it covered about ten acres of land and included wooden buildings constructed in 1808. The purpose of the Academy has always been to educate professional officers for the sea services.

In 1845 the minimum age for matriculation was thirteen and the maximum age sixteen. The staff in those days consisted of Commander Franklin Buchanan as the superintendent, four officers, and three civilian professors. There were about fifty midshipmen.

Today the Academy grounds cover over three hundred acres. The brigade of midshipmen consists of about four thousand men and women, and the faculty numbers some six hundred

United States Naval Academy Chapel

officers and civilians. Nineteen subjects are offered as majors, including engineering disciplines, the sciences, and the humanities. Graduates are awarded bachelor of science degrees and are commissioned ensigns in the United States Navy or second lieutenants in the United States Marine Corps.

The Academy's residence in Annapolis has been constant since its inception except for the period of the Civil War. Because of Southern sympathies in eastern Maryland and the uncertainty of the state joining the Confederacy in the early weeks of the war, it was deemed safer to move the school north. The famous frigate USS *Constitution*, then a school ship at Annapolis, transported the midshipmen to Newport, Rhode Island, in late April 1861. The faculty and equipment followed a week later aboard USS *Baltic*.

When the school was returned to Annapolis in 1865, the staff was dismayed to see the state of disrepair into which the Academy's buildings and grounds had fallen. The new superintendent, Rear Admiral David Dixon Porter, undertook major improvements to the physical facilities as well as the curriculum, athletic program, and social life. New Victorian quarters, classrooms, laboratories, and a chapel were constructed. The Maryland governor's house was purchased and used as the library. Over one hundred acres of adjoining property were added to the campus, providing orchards and fields for growing fresh vegetables for the mess hall. Steam engineering and advanced science became significant in the academic program. To expand the sports program, baseball, gymnastics, rowing, and boxing were added to fencing. Parades were held nearly every day except Sunday. There were so many social events that Annapolitans referred to the Academy as "Porter's dancing school." During the Spanish-American War, however, the importance of the Naval Academy became apparent, as its graduates were the senior naval leaders who were winning the smashing victories at sea.

Just before the Spanish American war, two studies had found the buildings at the Academy to be in poor condition and inadequate to support the needs of the Navy. Architect Ernest Flagg was hired to design and supervise construction of a "new" Naval Academy. He designed the present-day chapel, Bancroft Hall dormitory, the superintendent's house, the administration building, the library, and classroom buildings, arranging them around a central tree-shaded quadrangle with one side open to the Severn River. These buildings constitute the most outstanding ensemble of Beaux Arts buildings in the United States today. Flagg originally planned to convert the eighteenth-century Governor's Mansion back into a residence for the superintendent and to preserve the battery of old Fort Severn for a gymnasium. However, progress prevailed, and many of the old buildings were demolished. The library/mansion was razed to make room for the new armory, a new house was built for the superintendent, and Flagg had to sacrifice the boathouse for the new gymnasium, because the old battery was too small for the increasing student body.

The Naval Academy continued to grow and expand throughout the twentieth century. Between 1968 and 1991, a new line of classroom buildings as well as a library and an activities center were constructed overlooking the Severn River. They are modern in design, yet sensitive to Flagg's Beaux Arts scheme in their scale and detailing.

Dress parades take place on Worden Field, not far from the entrance at the Maryland Avenue Gate 3. Noon formations take place during good weather in Tecumseh Court in front of the massive Bancroft Hall dormitory. To begin a tour, visitors should enter through Gate 1 at the foot of King George Street and proceed to the Armel-Leftwich Visitors Center.

# Architectural Terms

*Adamesque.* Relating to the style of architecture and furniture designed by the brothers Robert and James Adam, eighteenth-century British architects.

*bay.* A main division of a structure; often used to describe the number of components in a building's facade.

*Beaux Arts.* Architectural style originating at the Ecole des Beaux Arts in Paris and popularized in the United States by "The Great White City" of the 1893 Columbian Exposition in Chicago. Classical in inspiration, Beaux Arts was symmetrical and employed Greco-Roman motifs. This style, much favored for public buildings, used stone as the preferred material.

*belt course.* A course (row) of brick or stone between the first and second (or second and third) stories of the building to give a more horizontal appearance. Also called a "string course."

*belvedere.* A roofed structure situated to command a view.

*bonding.* The pattern in which bricks are laid. During the colonial period there were several popular bonding styles: *English bond*—alternating courses (rows) of bricks, placed with the stretchers (long end) on one row, and the headers (short end) in the next row. *Flemish bond*—the placing of stretchers and headers alternately in the same row, and then alternating placement in the next row as well. *Header bond*—all rows on a face (side) of the building made up of the short end of the brick. Peculiar to Maryland and Virginia, header bond is seen only occasionally because of the large number of bricks required and the consequent expense. *Common bond* (also called *American bond*)—a course of headers followed by five to eight courses of stretchers before the use of another header row (post Revolution).

*Classical.* Architectural style patterned on that of ancient Greek and Roman architecture. Annapolis architecture reflects two different eras of classical influence: the neoclassical period, which encompasses Colonial and Federal architecture; and the Beaux Arts ascendancy at the beginning of the twentieth century.

*Colonial.* Architectural style prevailing in America during the colonial period; a modification of English Georgian.

*column.* A vertical support, usually cylindrical in form.

*cornice.* Uppermost part of the decoration nearest the roof (exterior) or the ceiling (interior).

*course.* A horizontal row of bricks or stones. *See also* bonding.

*cupola.* A small structure on top of the roof.

*curb roof.* A type of roof that has a ridge at the center and double slopes on each of its two sides.

*Doric.* Relating to the oldest, simplest of Greek architecture.

*dormer window.* Window projecting from a sloping roof.

*fanlight.* Semicircular window over a door with radiating bars in the form of a fan.

*English Regency.* Refers to the period between 1811 and 1820 (possibly extending to 1830). Characterized by elegant straight lines and restrained decoration.

*Federal.* Architectural style popular between 1785 and 1830 characterized by small-scale sophisticated detail and formal symmetry. Preferred materials were brick or frame.

*fenestration.* The arrangement of openings (windows and doors) in the facade of a building.

*French Second Empire.* Architectural style that flourished between 1860 and 1880 characterized by mansard roofs, formal symmetry, massive carriageways, and decorative ironwork.

*galleting.* Pebbles inlaid between stones to strengthen the large areas of mortar necessitated by the use of uncut stones. Usually seen in foundations (e.g., Brice House, Paca House) and often decorative in effect. Galleting is found in eighteenth- and nineteenth-century buildings in Annapolis but rarely in any other Maryland location.

*gambrel roof.* A gable roof, each side of which has a shallower slope above a steeper one. Today primarily used on barns.

*Georgian.* Architectural style prevalent in the English colonies from 1714 to 1776. Named after the four kings, George I through George IV, who ruled England starting in 1714.

*Georgian Revival.* A revival of the architectural style of the Georgian period (1714 to 1776) which took place in Annapolis primarily in the 1930s.

*gingerbread.* Ornaments executed with a jigsaw and placed under the eaves of the roof, so-called because of the resemblance to the frosting on gingerbread houses.

*Gothic Revival.* Architectural style featuring medieval details such as pointed arches. Popular in the United States between 1820 and 1860.

*Greek Revival.* Architectural style that flourished between 1820 and 1860 characterized by spare lines, temple fronts, and classical porticos, usually in the Doric and Ionic orders.

*hyphen.* A small building connecting two larger buildings; used as a passage from one to the other.

*hypocaust.* A type of underground heating system.

*Italianate or Villa.* Architectural style popular between 1840 and 1860 inspired by the medieval and Renaissance villas of Florence. Characterized by asymmetry, towers, arcades, and projecting eaves. Preferred materials were stucco and ashlar, a dressed stone used for facing brick and rubble walls.

*jib door.* A door to the garden. It may appear to be a full-length window and is sometimes disguised by continuing the decorations from the wall across the surface of the door.

*light.* Section of a window; a pane of glass.

*lintel.* A horizontal support beam, usually over a window or door but sometimes between two vertical pillars.

*Lombard Romanesque.* Style taken from the area of Lombardy, Italy, used in the Victorian period.

*mansard roof.* A form of curb roof whose lower slope nearly approaches the vertical and usually contains dormer windows, while the upper slope is nearly flat. Named after the French architects Francois and Jules Mansart, who used these roofs extensively at Versailles in the seventeenth century.

*modillions.* Ornamental brackets placed in series under the cornice.

*oriel window.* A bay window projecting from a wall.

*Palladian.* Architectural style named for Andrea Palladio, an Italian architect (1518–1580). Revived in England and the colonies in the eighteenth century.

*pediment.* In Classical architecture, the triangular-shaped gable area of a low-pitched roof, often filled with relief sculpture.

*pilaster.* A rectangular-shaped upright column set into a wall as an ornamental motif.

*Queen Anne.* Architectural style popular between 1880 and 1900, a revival of the style characteristic of the reign of Queen Anne of England (1701–1714). Usually combines brick, shingles, and half-timbering in asymmetrical assemblages to create picturesque profiles. Wrought iron and natural wood were used abundantly in this style.

*Romanesque Revival.* An architectural style inspired by European buildings of the ninth through the twelfth centuries, characterized by rounded arches, vaults, and heavy masonry construction. Popularized in the United States by the architect Henry Hobson Richardson between 1860 and 1890. St. Anne's Church is an example of the style as it appeared in northern Italy.

*sash.* Window frame.

*Second Empire. See* French Second Empire.

*shingle style.* Victorian period design, when shingles were cut and shaped in various forms to decorate building exteriors.

*spandrel.* The sometimes decorated triangular area between one side of an arch and the right angle formed by the horizontal element above and the vertical element alongside the arch.

*stick or carpenter.* Variant of the Queen Anne style characterized by elaborate wooden balustrades and other ornaments, often cut with a jigsaw.

*temple front.* Refers to the use of a classical temple form, with an elegant pediment over an impressive front door.

*Tudor.* Architecture developed during the reign of the Tudor family of England, from 1485 to 1603. The style is characterized by flat arches, shallow moldings, and a great variety of paneling on the walls, mostly of oak. There was a revival of this style in the Victorian period, 1840 to 1900.

*Tuscan.* Tuscany, being a part of Italy, contributed its own vernacular style of architecture to the Italian Villa style. The tower roof is rounded like a dome and is painted red to imitate clay tiles which would have crowned the top of an Italian building.

*Victorian.* In architecture, the term describes a number of style variations found during the reign of Queen Victoria in the nineteenth century.

*water table.* A horizontal projection of stone, brick, or wood below the first-floor level to shunt the rainwater away from the face of the building. There were no downspouts or gutters in the eighteenth century.

# Bibliography

Baltz, Shirley V. *The Quays of the City*. Annapolis: The Liberty Tree, 1975.

Barker, Charles Albro. *The Background of the Revolution in Maryland*. New Haven: Yale University Press, 1940.

Beirne, Rosamond R., and Edith R. Bevan. *The Hammond-Harwood House and Its Owners*. Rev. Ed. Annapolis: Hammond-Harwood House, 1954.

Bradford, James C. *Anne Arundel County, Maryland: A Bicentennial History, 1649–1977*. Annapolis: Anne Arundel County and Annapolis Bicentennial Committee, 1977.

Burdett, Harold N. *Yesteryear in Annapolis*. Cambridge, Md.: Tidewater Publishers, 1974.

Dozer, Donald Marquand. *Portrait of the Free State: A History of Maryland*. Cambridge, Md.: Tidewater Publishers, 1976.

Eddis, William. *Letters from America,* edited by Aubrey C. Land. Cambridge, Mass.: Harvard University Press, 1969.

Jackson, Elmer M., Jr. *Annapolis*. Annapolis: Capital-Gazette Press, 1936.

Lemay, A. J. Leo. *Men of Letters in Colonial Maryland*. Knoxville: University of Tennessee Press, 1972.

Miller, Marcia M., and Orlando Ridout V, eds. *Architecture in Annapolis: A Field Guide*. Crownsville, Md.: The Vernacular Architecture Forum and the Maryland Historical Trust Press, 2001.

Page, Jean Jepson. "Notes on the Contributions of Francis Blackwell Mayer and His Family to the Cultural History of Maryland." *Maryland Historical Magazine*, Vol. 76 (Fall 1981): 217–39.

Papenfuse, Edward C. *In Pursuit of Profit: The Annapolis Merchants in the Era of the American Revolution, 1763–1805*. Baltimore: Johns Hopkins University Press, 1975.

Paynter, William K. *St. Anne's Annapolis: History and Times*. Annapolis: St. Anne's Parish, 1980.

Riley, Elihu S. *"The Ancient City." A History of Annapolis, in Maryland. 1649–1887*. Annapolis, 1887. Reprint. Annapolis: Anne Arundel County and Annapolis Bicentennial Committee, 1977.

Stevens, William Oliver. *Annapolis: Anne Arundel's Town*. New York: Dodd, Mead, and Company, 1937.

United States Department of the Interior. *Historic American Buildings Survey*. Compiled and edited by National Park Service. Washington, D.C.: U.S. Department of the Interior, 1941.

Warren, Marion E., and Mame Warren. *An Annapolis Portrait, 1859–1910: "The Train's Done Been and Gone."* Rev. Ed. Annapolis: M. E. Warren, 1981.

———. *Everybody Works But John Paul Jones: A Portrait of the U. S. Naval Academy, 1845–1915*. Annapolis: Naval Institute Press, 1981.

Wehr, Frederick T. *Flags and Seals of Maryland and of the United States*. Baltimore: National Society of the Colonial Dames of America in the State of Maryland, 1975.

# Index

The principal description of a building or a site is indicated in italic type; an asterisk denotes a building no longer extant.

## C

**P**

**R**

**S**